"From his years of leading young adults, planting a thriving and successful local congregation, and leading in care and development for clergy in a denomination, Steve Ely has produced a discipleship resource that touches the core of how our lives are changed by the Word and Spirit of God. This is a must-read for all interested in drawing closer to Jesus and changing our generation."

**Presiding Bishop A.D. Beacham, Jr.**
**General Superintendent IPHC**

"Steve's years of ministry experience as an Evangelist, Youth Pastor, denominational Youth/Young Adult Ministry Director, Church Planter, Lead Pastor, and now, Director of Clergy Development for his denomination, along with life experiences have fueled Steve's desire to help people make the most of their time on earth as disciples of Christ. His passion for discipleship and forming people is evident as you read this book. Pastors, the seventeen Kingdom Characteristics that he biblically and practically develops would make a great sermon/Bible study series. Youth pastors/young adult leaders, this would make a great discipleship series for those you are mentoring in the faith.

I have known Steve since he was student at Southwestern Christian University in Oklahoma City, Oklahoma. Later, while serving as the Executive Director of IPHC Church Education Ministries, now Discipleship Ministries, Steve served as the Director of Youth/Young Adult Ministries. Today, we both find ourselves back at the Global Ministry Center/IPHC.

Steve remains one of the most passionate, articulate, and competent Ministry Directors/Leaders that I have had the privilege of serving and serving with. I have always listened and weighed what he has to say, and you and I would be wise to let the truths shared in this book transform our hearts."

**Bishop Talmadge Gardner**
**World Missions Ministries IPHC**
**Executive Director**

"My friend Steve Ely has crafted a text with powerful content and impact using a most unusual metaphor. As only a native and resident of

Oklahoma could do, he uses the weather to provide incredible biblical truths and principles. The uniqueness and imagery of his writing style are entertaining and engaging.

Drawing from his own Christian journey and ministry experience gives this read an amazing level of insight and personal application. This book is a must read for the individual believer and a great tool for those who are privileged to assist others in their walk of faith.

After reading *Climate Change*, Romans chapter 12 will never be the same. Thanks, Pastor Steve, for this gift to me and the body of Christ."

**Bishop Garry Bryant**
**Evangelism USA IPHC**
**Executive Director**

"I love variations in weather and the causes. Without the Call, I could have been a weather forecaster. Spiritually, perhaps I am. I love this book and am intrigued by the comparisons of climate/weather and the spiritual journey. The text is like a magnet. The attracted reader is hooked, inspired, and taught. The book is refreshingly Biblical. The reader certainly cannot desire a certain weather environment without having developed a prior corresponding climate. I highly recommend the book for one's personal journey and for teaching in a small group setting. The book begs for discussion. I will teach it. One's climate can be changed. Good weather can be found. Read the book! Well done, Pastor."

**President D. Chris Thompson**
**Holmes Bible College**

"Steve Ely is an outstanding storyteller with a penchant for a clever turn-of-phrase, but don't miss the wisdom of a man with decades in the trenches of loving, serving, and leading God's people. *Climate Change* is a great reminder to Christians everywhere to deal with destructive patterns and chaotic cycles by getting to the root of the problem—renewing our mind and conforming it to the measure of Christ. Don't get angry about the weather; change your life by changing the climate."

**Stephen Jones**
**Director of Student Ministries IPHC**

"I am very excited about Steve Ely's book *Climate Change*. For many years, my friend Steve has preached and lived out the principles in each powerful chapter. After reading it, I am stirred again to live in the Kingdom Climate. I highly recommend it!"

**Terry Lowder**
**Chief of Staff and Assistant to the General Superintendent IPHC**

"Steve Ely, having reached the stage of life where spiritual maturity and life experiences merge, writes *Climate Change*. He is a son of Oklahoma, living most of his life in this region. Maybe the people of this state are more conscious of weather, weather patterns, and climate than any other. I get it. After living more than ten years in Oklahoma, I am immersed in the "pastime, hobby" of paying close attention to weather news and climate issues.

How meaningful that Ely frames his Biblical teaching around weather and climate patterns. Romans 12:3-21 is the passage where he focuses his "spiritual Doppler radar." He shares 17 characteristics presented by the writer Paul to emphasize the great need to grasp the Kingdom climate that Jesus wants to grow in our lives. The long-term changes in our minds create the climate of our lives.

I highly commend the writing of this book and recommend this for anyone interested in following Jesus."

**Dr. Lou Shirey**
**Director of Thriving in Ministry**
**International Pentecostal Holiness Church**

"As a lifelong Georgia resident, I have often remarked to those around me, "If you like the weather in Georgia, don't worry…it will change!" In Climate Change, Steve Ely boldly challenges us to discern the differences between temporary recurrent weather and the bigger picture of climate as it relates to cultural trends, global concerns, and human behavior. As followers of Jesus, we need to be more focused on the root causes underneath our actions and attitudes to discern the mindset and worldviews supporting the behaviors. Steve vividly describes the kind of climate God is endeavoring as he expresses his kingdom on planet Earth through his followers. But it's not enough to know the difference; we must have the courage to change the climate. I believe this is a message for our generation not only to hear and understand but also to heed and practice. Steve Ely helps us become better thermostats and not simply thermometers as we affect deeply embedded spiritual change in our local and global climate."

**Dr. C. Tracy Reynolds**
**Campus Pastor, Grace Fellowship Madison, Georgia**

# CLIMATE CHANGE

*God's Plan For Calming Life's Storms*

STEVE ELY

Copyright © 2024 Steve Ely All rights reserved.

No part of this publication may be reproduced, stored, or transmitted in any form or by any means, including written, copied, or electronically, without prior written permission from the author or his agents. The only exception is brief quotations in printed reviews. Short excerpts may be used with the publisher's or author's expressed written permission.

**Climate Change:**

Cover and Interior Page design by True Potential, Inc.

ISBN: (Paperback): 9781960024343

ISBN: (e-book): 9781960024350

LCCN: 2024930787

True Potential, Inc.

PO Box 904, Travelers Rest, SC 29690

www.truepotentialmedia.com

Cover and Interior Page design by True Potential, Inc.

## CONTENTS

| | |
|---|---|
| Acknowledgments | 9 |
| Foreword | 13 |
| 1. Climate Confusion | 15 |
| 2. Storm Chasers | 21 |
| 3. Forecasts | 27 |
| 4. Wind Comes Sweeping Down The Plains | 31 |
| 5. Porches and Pigs | 37 |
| 6. The Rest of The Story | 41 |
| 7. Connect Four (Actually more) | 47 |
| 8. In It To Win It! | 55 |
| 9. What's Love Got To Do With It? | 61 |
| 10. Play Your Cards Right! | 67 |
| 11. Live Like You Are In The Movies! | 73 |
| 12. On Your Feet! | 77 |
| 13. I Am Disneyland! | 83 |
| 14. Pain Partners | 91 |
| 15. Wall Wars | 97 |
| 16. Grin and Share It! | 105 |
| 17. Belly Button Theology | 113 |
| 18. Your Feet Clean? | 121 |
| 19. You Don't Look Good In Green! | 125 |
| 20. Major vs. Minor | 131 |

| | |
|---|---|
| 21. Sandpaper and Songs | 137 |
| 22. Crossing the Line? | 141 |
| 23. Let It Go, Let it Go! | 145 |
| 24. Dig It! | 151 |
| About the Author | 155 |

# ACKNOWLEDGMENTS

It was a ritual. Sunday after Sunday, as a teenager, we would wait for the last amen to be said at our church in Apache, Oklahoma. Crammed into Les' old blue car or Johnny's Silverado truck or Z24 coupe and head to the nearest "big" town to go to the mall. After we grabbed a quick bite to eat, we made our way to the real destination. It was called the "Salt Cellar". It was a tiny Christian bookstore tucked in the corner of the mall. Equally tucked away in the bookstore was a back wall lined with cassette players (if you know, you know) with headphones and racks of the latest contemporary Christian music. We spent hours and literally thousands of dollars purchasing what we thought was the soundtrack of our youth. Bands like Degarmo and Key, Petra, Stryper, Farrell and Farrell, Servant, Sweet Comfort Band, Mylon Lefevre, and Broken Heart, and artists like Leon Pattillo, Bryan Duncan, Russ Taff, Darrell Mansfield, just to name a few, were evaluated and then wrapped up to take home.

The truth is these tunes I thought were just for my youth are the soundtrack of my life. I still listen to them daily. The journey to get the music was only part of the ritual for me. As I listened to the music, I would carefully remove the liner notes and meticulously read every word of the acknowledgments the artists included. Most people I knew only bought the music to listen to the music. However, I wanted to read the "why" and "who" behind the tunes. Who influenced the artist to write? Why was the music important to the singer? I still practice this ritual today, but only now, it is with books. I know most people view the acknowledgment pages as something to hurriedly skip or maybe even a waste of pages. However, for me, it provides a necessary glimpse into what made the author. That is what the following people have done for me. They made me. If it weren't for those listed here, the weather of my life would have eventually destroyed me. These folks helped shape and form the climate of my life that has ultimately produced the weather of wholeness. To them and those that I may have missed, I am forever grateful.

Apache 1st Pentecostal Holiness Church - what a divine place to grow up and learn to love Jesus. I have spent my entire life trying to find and even build a church like you. In my mind and heart, you set the standard that every other church must live up to. With people like Cecil and Marie McClure, Leroy and Charlene Hise, Fred and Ann Orf, Roy and JoAnn Palesano, Bob and Kay Muse, Kent "Z" and Freddie Palesano, and scores of others, how could anyone ever live up to them?

Southwestern Christian University - Your influence on my life is immeasurable. Living and working on campus gave me lifelong friends and training that I still draw on to this day.

McColl Pentecostal Holiness Church and The Pulse Youth - I cut my ministry teeth on you. You taught me way more than I taught you. Thanks for being patient with a rookie.

Greenville First and RASORS Youth - We didn't really know what we had built until our young people grew up. You are the trophies of our lives. You have proven that youth ministry matters and that God can use people who don't have a clue what they are doing.

Pastors John and Marjorie Palesano, Pastors Dan and Sandy Palesano, Pastors Buddy and Wanda Lampley, Pastors Frank and Betty Gentry, Pastors David and Sandy Wood, Pastors Richard and Linda Goad - I am standing on your shoulders.

Authors and preachers like Jamie Buckingham, Max Lucado, Gene Edwards, Dr. Dharius Daniels, and so many others whom I may never meet in person but have spoken life into my soul.

Dad and Mom #1 - I am forever indebted to you. You made the choice to break the weather pattern that could have impacted our family for generations. Your faithfulness to one another and absolute dedication to Jesus will continue to impact generations to come. You built the right climate

# ACKNOWLEDGMENTS

for that to happen. You are my heroes. Because of you and the name you have established, I am rich.

Calvin and Louise Upton (Dad and Mom #2) - Your home was a safe place for me. Being grafted into the Upton family is one of my greatest treasures in life.

Pastors Bud and Shari Jones (Dad and Mom #3) - Your undying and unwavering belief in me shaped me. The best church needed the best pastors, and that's what we got when we got you. You modeled what pastors should be like. You are the gold standard that very few ever live up to.

Les and B.Kay Jones, and Johnny and Kristy Upton - You are the reason they are called "best" friends. I am and always will be your Tonto!

Paul and Mary Howell, Dr. Doug and Susan Beacham, Talmadge and Stephanie Gardner - Thank you for trusting me to lead and believing that I could actually do it.

Joe and Becky Francisco and Kelly Clarke, Charles, and Laura Boyd - Lifers! Your consistent presence in our lives has meant more than you will ever know.

Passion Church - Together, we lived this book. I still can't believe you were willing to call me pastor and that you were willing to follow. Together, we did the hard work of building Kingdom Climate. I believe that it was worth the price we paid. You are our pride and joy. We are thankful for your trust and friendship.

Compassion Network, Josh Hannah, John Leggett, and all the pastors in my region who helped us walk through some stormy weather and let us lean on you until we found health and sunny days.

Danny Nix and Warren Beemer - My brothers and my friends, you made me better. I miss you daily.

Julie - When I try to imagine my life without you, I can't. Without you, the weather of my life would have produced destruction. Now, even on rainy days, I am not afraid because you are with me. I love you!

Tal, Kelley, and Devin - That God trusted us with you is a miracle. You are the best of us. My prayer is that Mom and I have taught and modeled for you the climate described in this book. We didn't and don't always get it right, but hopefully, we showed you that it is possible to live like this! Our prayer is that you will work to construct the same climate in your lives and homes. I love you!

Steve Spillman, Chris Maxwell, and Kristi Cain - Thanks for pushing me to finish this book and editing it to make sure it makes sense. I am grateful for your efforts, but even more for your friendship.

Reader - I hope you will enjoy this book. However, I pray that you will be challenged by this book. I pray that as you read, you will commit to doing the hard work of establishing a Kingdom Climate in your life.

Finally, Jesus, I realize that I don't deserve you. I am daily reminded of Your continued great grace. I relate to Degarmo and Key's song, "Here's to all the losers, lose all guilt and sin. Here's to life in Jesus, where all of the losers win." I am a loser who won because of you, Jesus!

# FOREWORD

So much is happening in our personal lives, in our churches, in our communities, in our nation, in our world. What can we do about it? What should we do about it? What will we do about it?

We can respond in several ways.

Many choose to sit and watch this show of life. Accepting the role of victims, these people complain and find fault and critique. They know what should be done and let everyone know everything they know should be done. But they do nothing. Just watching and griping, often using biblical reasons to grumble. They are miserable. Waiting for Jesus to come, they choose to battle with words and attitudes only. Action isn't on their agenda.

Others choose to help problems and disasters become realities. Attack appears to be their purpose. Conversations and situations and relationships and circumstances are all seen as battles. Wars to be won. Opponents to be defeated. These people seek to find a storm. They cherish predicted and expected derailment. They bring them to life.

Some, however, choose to take a biblical tactic. They see hope in the confusion. They live with faith amid the doubt and division. They welcome truth, unity, compassion, conviction, and commitment. They choose to proclaim truth amid all the confusion. They hear an invitation from the Holy Spirit to impact the world with hope.

That is the invitation Steve Ely is offering us in Climate Change.

Steve isn't afraid to speak the truth. He does that with his sermons and his conversations. He does that with his words on these pages. He refuses to sit back and just watch things happen. Neither is he willing to become someone hoping for the worst. Instead, he sees our present situations. He refuses to waver from biblical truth. And he offers this book as his own conversation with us amid all the storms of life.

Why? Why is Steve taking this stand and inviting us to join him?

Because he believes the stories he tells and the sermons he proclaims are truth. He believes today's culture is desperate for that truth. And Steve takes us there on these pages—giving us a glance at our culture, ourselves, and our beliefs. We visit the wind sweeping down the plains. We ride harsh waves with names like cancer, bankruptcy, divorce, and death. We seek to be calm, to be still, but the world is rushing us too many places to do what doesn't really matter.

We need, instead, to connect. To serve. To love. To flee evil and cling to what is good.

Steve Ely's words offer us those reminders and hand us deep questions. Will we settle for t-shirts and bumper stickers, cool goals, and new agendas? Will we rejoice as a movement selects a catchy theme to count our improvements? Will the new loud worship song make everything better?

Or is there more?

Will we transform into a kingdom climate? Will we become part of the narrative offering true transformation?

I hope so. I pray so. And I believe we can. I believe the time is now. The time is now to not settle for the climate but rather to change what is into what it should become. We will begin hearing different comments, notice better updates, and see miraculous stories.

As Steve writes, "Miracles almost always reside on the other side of obedience." Let us believe and receive that. Let us obey. Let us get ready for the spiritual climate to change. Let it begin, through us, today.

**Chris Maxwell**

**Pastor, Author, Spiritual Life Director Emmanuel University**

# 1. CLIMATE CONFUSION

The sun disappeared. The sirens sounded. It appeared out of troubled, swirling, dark clouds like a massive destructive felt-tipped marker, dropped out of the sky, and left its ugly black mark on the countryside. The dilemma was the stroke wasn't reserved just for the countryside. The funnel, 300 miles per hour winds, and rain turned and came into the densely populated city of Moore, Oklahoma. The path was apparent and violent. The seventeen-mile-long and 1.3-mile-wide swath of destruction was outlined with the litter of uprooted trees, mangled automobiles, leveled houses, and debris.

There are absolutely no words that can do justice to the scene. My wife, Julie, and I rode in the back of a pickup handing out hot meals and were struck speechless. Our minds struggled to compute, much less comprehend, the devastation. Our eyes widened, and our jaws dropped at the site of house-high piles of shattered wood and shingles. There were automobiles that were twisted and impaled by trees. Private and personal belongings were scattered and tattered as far as the eyes could see. People, like zombies, meandered aimlessly through the streets. It was like they wanted to run and hide, but now there was nothing to which they could run.

The ruin was complete, and yet it was also random. Entire city blocks lay bare to the foundations, then right in the middle of havoc, a single house entirely spared with dishes still unmoved on shelves. The property loss was mind-numbing, but it was the loss of life that did the most damage. The May 2013 tornado was one of the deadliest in history. It claimed the lives of twenty-four people. The next storm was one of anger, disbelief, and the rallying cry for change because of the twenty-four lives lost (nine were children). The storm was bad. The tornado's timing was worse. It descended just as schools were letting out for the day. One elementary school took a direct hit. The result? Seven children lost forever in the rubble of the unrecognizable hallways.

The Nation watched as sobbing parents and friends were sifting through the wreckage, trying to unearth their children. They were hoping against hope that their most prized possessions were only buried briefly rather than permanently. The guttural wails of those who received the most dreaded news were haunting. Almost simultaneously, after the final count of those who were lost was posted and reported, it began. Rallies were held, petitions were signed, legislators made speeches, and money began to flow in to make change. A movement began. A demand was made to ensure there was never a repeat performance of this tragedy. The solution offered was that every school in the State would be equipped with a "Safe Room" or "Storm Shelter" capable of withstanding the vicious winds of a tornado. Millions of dollars were raised. Schools miles away from the destruction altered their upcoming building plans. The schools that were destroyed on that fateful May day have been reconstructed with these types of safe havens in place.

Interestingly enough, for all the speeches about making it possible to survive one of these deadly storms, there was no talk about how to stop them. No campaign was launched to figure out how never to have another tornado. No bill passed for federal studies on how to curtail tornadic activity. Survival was the rallying cry. Enduring was the ultimate goal. Schemes were rolled out to enable folks to ride out the weather and live another day.

Unfortunately, it appears that this same desire for survival and endurance has invaded our lives as believers. While climate change in the natural is debatable, in the spiritual realm, it can sometimes seem impossible. Therefore, there seems to be little talk of stopping storms, but bookshelves and pulpits are flooded with instructions on how to hold on, survive, batten down the hatches, grit your teeth, clench your fist, make it through, and simply persevere. In our longing for temporary relief, significant change is forgotten. This has caused two major issues to blow into our lives.

The first issue is that we confuse climate and weather. Climate and weather are not the same thing. Webster's Dictionary defines climate as "a significant and lasting change in the statistical distribution of weather patterns over periods ranging from decades to millions of years." So, climate is more than weather! Climate is, in fact, what sets weather into motion. Climate controls weather. Climate dictates what the weather will be. One of the problems with confusing climate and weather is it causes us to rail against weather. We beat our chests in anger about the storm we are facing. We shake our fists at God for allowing the weather. While we cry, accuse, and grow bitter, we refuse, or more specifically, allow Jesus or the Holy Spirit, to address the climate of our lives that produces the weather pattern we hate.

> THE FIRST ISSUE IS THAT WE CONFUSE CLIMATE AND WEATHER. CLIMATE AND WEATHER ARE NOT THE SAME THING.

When you confuse climate and weather, the other tendency is to celebrate momentary breaks in the weather as if a significant change has taken place. We applaud lulls in the chaos. We hold our breath amid a month-long calm, hoping that nothing will mess it up. However, it is inevitable! Without climate change, the storms will re-form and recycle. Even though we were shocked and dumbfounded when the storms blew back in again one month later, two years later, or 20 years later, we knew that they would because we never addressed climate.

The truth is that most of us are really just fighting and enduring the same storm we have been fighting for years. The depression we faced when we were 15 years old now rumbles back around when we are twenty-five. It is just a new version... depression 2.0. The addiction endured at 14 years old, seemingly out of nowhere, rushes back in with all of its thunder and high winds when we are forty-five. It is just addiction 3.0. We continue to face the weather that our climate produces. The inability to distinguish between the two and the unwillingness to do the incredibly hard work of addressing climate keeps us in stormy weather. When you live in Oklahoma, you know to expect tornadoes because our climate is conducive to them. If you make your home in Florida, you won't be surprised when a hurricane is on the horizon. In the natural, we know that climate dictates the weather. We must come to an understanding that if we aren't willing to address the climate of our lives, then we shouldn't be shocked, surprised, or even angered by the weather that continues to develop! Our climate dictates our weather.

The second major issue is perhaps even more devastating. Because we confuse climate and weather, we want to turn Jesus into a weather forecaster. In Oklahoma, meteorologists are rock stars. They are literally autograph-signing, picture-taking celebrities. Although I appreciate their ability to give us warnings about approaching storms (we will talk about forecasting later), beyond that, they have no power! They simply study patterns and try to prepare us for the weather. When we confuse climate and weather, that is what we do with Jesus. We simply want Him to prepare us for bad weather. Some of us will allow Him to go one step further. We graduate and relegate Him to being the fixer.

Do you remember the movie "Karate Kid"? No . . . not the terrible remake from a few years ago. The good one. The original one. The one that caused you to get martial arts lessons and stand on one leg with your arms raised above your head like a praying mantis. You know you did that! Do you remember the storyline? Daniel LaRusso and his single mom, with a new job in hand and in an attempt to escape the rough neighborhoods of New Jersey, move to Reseda, California. Instead of the plush house with a swimming pool that Daniel had been promised, they moved into a rundown apartment complex.

Daniel has an encounter with a small Asian maintenance man named Mr. Miyagi. When something was broken in the apartment, Daniel would call on Mr. Miyagi. If the dishwasher or doorknob didn't work, he would call Mr. Miyagi. Mr. Miyagi would fix the broken item. Then Daniel would dismiss him. That is what we do to Jesus when we don't understand climate. We ask Him to come to our rescue and to fix things that are broken. Because He loves us, He responds and repairs, and then we send Him away. The only problem is the new stuff breaks, and the old stuff breaks again. Fixed hearts shatter again. Repaired relationships rupture again. Replenished bank accounts tend to empty quickly again! So, each and every time, we call for the fixer to come back. Daniel's relationship with Mr. Miyagi was like that until that night!

You remember that night, don't you? Daniel is walking next to the beautiful girl he met at school. The dance is over. His crush has caused Daniel to focus his attention on her. He should have been focused on his surroundings. Daniel finds himself surrounded by the members of the Cobra Kai Martial Arts Club. They don't like Daniel. They had already warned him to leave this girl alone. They constantly bullied him at school. It is very apparent that Daniel is about to be beaten unmercifully. Suddenly, out of nowhere, the fixer shows up in a blurry flash of speed and dexterity. Mr. Miyagi saves the day and Daniel's face. Suddenly, Daniel has a revelation! He has underestimated and failed to discern this little Asian maintenance man. Mr. Miyagi is more than a fixer! He is instead a sensei . . . a teacher. We, too, must have a similar revelation about Jesus. Does Jesus have the power to fix? Absolutely! Does He have the ability to mend? Thankfully, yes. Does He have the strength to enable us to survive the weather? YES!! But the revelation that can set us free is that Jesus isn't just a fixer and certainly isn't just a weatherman. I am so thankful that He is an anchor in the storm. However, the revelation we must receive is that Jesus is The Teacher who can teach us how to stop the storm once and for all. Rather than fighting the same weather patterns for the rest of our lives, we must allow Jesus to teach us how to forecast, address, and control climate so that weather forever changes.

> RATHER THAN FIGHTING THE SAME WEATHER PATTERNS FOR THE REST OF OUR LIVES, WE MUST ALLOW JESUS TO TEACH US HOW TO FORECAST, ADDRESS, AND CONTROL CLIMATE.

The goal is to establish "Kingdom Climate" so that we begin to experience "Kingdom Weather"! Be warned, climate change is hard. There are days when bad weather seems more desirable than the pain of making the necessary adjustments, cuts, and choices required to experience Jesus as a Climate-Changer. In *The Bait of Satan*, John Bevere says, "We are rooted and grounded when we bear this intense love and trust in God. No storm, no matter how intense, can ever move us. This does not come by strong will or personality. It is a gift of grace to all who place their confidence in God, throwing away the confidence of self. But to give yourself in total abandonment, you must know the One who holds your life."

Since we know The Teacher, Jesus, holds our life, we must also know that we can trust Him to help us through the painful moments, necessary cuts, and stormy, thunder-filled days. We can relinquish our preferences and our belief in our own abilities to make the necessary climate changes on our own. This allows us to lean on Him so that we walk, with His help, into new weather produced by the change in climate. That kind of change is worth every tear and fear!

## 2. STORM CHASERS

It is burned into my memory. I can't get the picture out of my head. I was probably five or six years old. I was standing in a dark, musty underground cellar, and the sheets of rain falling outside were also making their way into the safe haven. I was standing in water up to my shins. My mom was huddled with me and my sister because the dreaded shrieking of the tornado siren had motivated us to take shelter. My dad stood at the top of the concrete steps leading to the underground shelter. I could see over his shoulder, and what I saw was terrifying and beautiful at the same time. Three tornadoes lowering out of the sky headed our way.

I remember my mom hollering at my dad to join us in the cellar, but he continued to stand there and watch as the sky darkened and the funnels neared. I am not sure why he stood there rather than joining us in safety, but I remember thinking how brave he was. (Truth be told, I do the same now. My wife and boys run to the cellar, and I stand outside staring into the sky. I guess it is just what dads do.) However, as brave as my dad was, he wasn't a storm chaser.

You may not even realize there are such beings. Still, there are card-carrying, iron-clad car-driving, dashboard-camera-using crazies that actually and intentionally chase down tornadoes and try to get as close to them as possible. That is a whole "nother" level of brave (or nuts)! They don't just watch at a safe distance like my dad. Instead, they run headlong into the path of the storm. They take trucks and weld extra panels of steel on them until they look like some alien ship just to help them withstand the driving hail and flying debris they encounter as they get as close to the storm as possible. It is almost as if they enjoy the nasty weather that surrounds them. In fact, they capitalize on it. They get paid to video the funnel and to send a bird's-eye view back to weather forecasters and the audience watching on TV. Apparently, storm chasing is a very old profession. These same guys were around even in Jesus' day!

I can't prove it, but when Jesus arrived on the scene, I bet the house was surrounded by chariots with extra, hail-resistant iron panels attached to them that made their ride look all space-shippy. They had beaten Jesus to the storm, or maybe the truth is, they had brought the storm with them. A broken mom and dad had just begun grieving their dead daughter. Mind-reeling. Heart-shattered. Incredible loss. Hope gone. Laughter was a memory. It is THE storm of storms for any parent. Parents are not supposed to outlive their children. Then Jesus shows up. However, remember, Jesus is more than a weatherman. He is commissioned and assigned to change the climate. It is interesting to see Jesus jump the fence, Mr. Miyagi-style, of despair and fly into action. When Jesus entered the synagogue leader's house and saw the noisy crowd (the disorderly crowd) and people playing pipes (one version says these are people who make music for funerals), *He said, "Go away. The girl is not dead, but asleep." But, they laughed at Him* (The King James Version says, "*They laughed him to scorn.*"). *After the crowd had been put outside* (this is too docile in English - in the original, it has a "forcibly thrown" out feel), *He went in and took the girl by the hand, and she got up.* (Matthew 9:18-19, 23-25 NIV)

The Message Bible may more clearly reveal the account.

Matthew 9:23-24 (MSG)

> *By now they had arrived at the house of the town official, and pushed their way through the gossips looking for a story and the neighbors bringing in casseroles. Jesus was abrupt: "Clear out! This girl isn't dead. She's sleeping." They told him he didn't know what he was talking about.*

Jesus didn't mess around. He was abrupt. He instantly, intentionally, and yes, even forcibly took control of the climate. This isn't how we do things. We first deal with the weather ... the storm ... the death. We console and attempt to convince grievers that though the weather is bad, they will get used to it in time. Jesus ignored the weather and attacked the climate. Jesus dramatically shows us that for there to be climate change, there must first be climate control. Said another way, "Climate Control must precede Climate Change!"

The storm chasers are in full funeral mode. Cries of anguish fill the air. The room is full of doubt, disbelief, and death. These are card-carrying storm chasers. These folks really don't care about the great loss this family has suffered. They have no memories of a young girl learning to ride her bike or pulling on their heartstrings and demanding wails of sorrow. There is no mourning because of the potential that has been forfeited. Oh, their sound was sad, and their faces were marked with tears, but there was no emotional investment. These folks who were mourning, playing music, and making a scene in accordance and compliance with the custom of that day were paid mourners. This was a paid gig. This was their job. This was their profession. And they were good at it! So, prior to operating in the gift of healing, Jesus operates in the gift of hater removal. He removed the storm chasers. They had to be forcibly removed, not because they cared, but because they would lose their check if they vacated. Jesus cleared the house! He didn't wait for it to clear. He didn't wait for people to wander out that needed to be kicked out!

> JESUS OPERATES IN THE GIFT OF HATER REMOVAL. HE REMOVED THE STORM CHASERS.

Jesus instantly recognized that before there could be any change and before the weather would change, He had to deal with the climate that the doubters, the scoffers, and the unbelievers brought with them. He knew that the haters had to exit. Jesus was decisive about this. The climate was disorderly, and He is a God who operates in order. The climate was chaos, and He is a God that doesn't operate in confusion. He knew that He could not call something "sleep" if everyone else in the room was calling it "death"! So, He steps in and controls the climate.

This is a lesson that we must learn. Too many of us are asking for climate change, yet we are unwilling to control the climate. You can long for a change to righteousness, but if you won't control the climate of filth around you, there will be no change. You can learn financial principles and long for financial freedom, and you will continue to suffer with overwhelming debt if you don't deal with the climate of stewardship, which forces us to address overspending and obedience in tithing. Trying to change the weather to blessing while ignoring the climate of disobedience and rebellion is futile. Rail against the weather of broken relationships all you want. However, if we refuse to address the climate of physical intimacy before marriage, our brokenness, anger, a sharp tongue, and selfishness, the weather cycle will continue. Pray for peace to replace our life full of constant turmoil, but if we don't deal with the climate of double-mindedness, then chaos will be our constant companion. Lonely, and we wonder why. Yet, we are unwilling to confront the climate of standoffishness and suspicion that surrounds our lives. Jesus' actions at this moment teach us that climate control will sometimes dictate dismissal.

Unfortunately, there are storm chasers in all of our lives. These folks make a profession out of celebrating the death that we are living through. They are pros! These are people who profit from our pain. These people bank on our brokenness. There are people who consistently and confidently fill the room of our lives with mourning, chaos, and noise. These folks are rooting for our death and resisting our life because, if we get healed, it reveals the sickness and death in their own life. They are so comfortable and dependent on our current condition that they could not handle a change and are intentionally working against it. The truth is there are people trying to convince us something is dead when it is only asleep. They say the dream is dead, but it is only asleep. They read the last rites over our future, declaring it to be dead, but it is only asleep. They write the obituary for our marriage and dig the hole for burial when the relationship and vows really just need to be dusted off, grabbed by the hand and walked into new life.

Jesus' encounter with storm chasers reveals that in order to control your climate, you must come to grips with the fact that you will lose more people during ascension than you ever did when you were descending. He teaches us that everyone deserves love, but not everyone has earned access! Your change will come when you do more than just put them off but rather take the climate-changing step of putting them out. Following Paul's admonishment to live in peace with everyone, you may need to prayerfully allow the Holy Spirit to give you wisdom about who needs less access to your life. This may mean that you will need to dismiss folks. It may require you to take the painful and heart-wrenching steps necessary to get them or at least their influence out of your life. You may have to delete their number. Unfriend or unfollow them online. Give them no access. This lack of access may be for a season. It could potentially last longer. However, if you don't dismiss . . . life will not and cannot come. If you don't gain distance from them, then they will cheer you right back into confusion. They will freak you right back into falling. They will dance you right back into distraction and destruction. It is time to turn the tables on them and chase the storm chasers! Walk them to their indestructible cars and send them packing. They will easily find another storm to celebrate . . . it is their job.

# 3. FORECASTS

They come in all varieties. Two days. Four days. Seven days and sometimes even fourteen days. We make plans with them. A day at the lake is rescheduled before the first drop of rain is ever felt. A road trip is moved up before the first sign of slick spots. Schools cancel classes, and Walmart shelves are emptied of bread and milk before a single snowflake enters the atmosphere. All of these choices and actions are based on forecasts. Complicated radars, calculations, and million-dollar computers work to predict the weather before it arrives so that we know how to plan, pack the right clothes, and prepare alternate routes. Forecasting is defined like this by Webster's Dictionary. . . "to calculate or predict (some future event or condition) usually as a result of study and analysis of available pertinent data." Pertinent data is often obvious but overlooked. However, the observant among us carefully analyze and pay attention to indicators that point to a discernible end. Jesus was the master forecaster.

One account of Jesus' forecasting ability is found in John 8.

John 8:1-11 (TLB)

> *Jesus returned to the Mount of Olives, but early the next morning, he was back again at the Temple. A crowd soon gathered, and he sat down and taught them. As he was speaking, the teachers of religious law and the Pharisees brought a woman who had been caught in the act of adultery. They put her in front of the crowd. "Teacher," they said to Jesus, "this woman was caught in the act of adultery. The law of Moses says to stone her. What do you say?" They were trying to trap him into saying something they could use against him, but Jesus*

*stooped down and wrote in the dust with his finger. They kept demanding an answer, so he stood up again and said, "All right, but let the one who has never sinned throw the first stone!" Then he stooped down again and wrote in the dust. When the accusers heard this, they slipped away one by one, beginning with the oldest, until only Jesus was left in the middle of the crowd with the woman. Then Jesus stood up again and said to the woman, "Where are your accusers? Didn't even one of them condemn you?" "No, Lord," she said. And Jesus said, "Neither do I. Go and sin no more."*

Verse 11 (NIV): "*No one, Master.*" "*Neither do I,*" *said Jesus.* "*Go on your way. From now on, don't sin.*"

Verse 11 (MSG): "*Well, I do not condemn you either; all I ask is that you go and from now on avoid the sins that plague you.*"

We read this account, and our attention is drawn to the evident and incredible mercy and forgiveness that Jesus extends to this broken woman! We read and haggle over details that are omitted and cause our imagination to run wild. What did Jesus write in the dirt? Where was the man who was caught in the act with this woman? We hone in on topics like judgment, hypocrisy, and sexism (where was the man the woman was with?). The truth is this account does highlight all of those themes. However, we miss that this encounter reveals Jesus' ability to accurately and precisely read the climate to forecast future weather!

Severe humiliation and shame. She has been called out and paraded in front of everyone. The bright red of her face travels quickly south to her hands (She was caught red-handed). In the act! Jesus' sharp and absolutely brilliant response to her accusers causes arrogance to be abandoned. Tear gas couldn't have caused them to disperse more effectively or expediently. Looking up from His sand sketch, Jesus asks this lady where the "rock band" went. She informs her Savior that they have gone on to another gig. With the storm chasers dismissed, Jesus reverses the death sentence she had received from the church folks. "Neither do I condemn you!" That is an important and life-giving statement. However, it is the next five forecasting words that may be an even more important statement. With no fancy computer graphics or animated sun, lightning bolts, or raindrops layered over the green screen behind Him, Jesus gives this woman a forecast of her life. He says, "Go and sin no more!" These words reveal that the climate you allow or operate in forecasts your future. I believe Jesus is saying to this woman, "Listen, if you don't deal with the climate of your life, then the sin that got you here will bring you right back here. Although I was here to rescue you this time, I may not be here to run these guys off the second time! Either change your climate or destruction is inevitable. If we would simply allow Jesus to point to the radar of our life, then we would see patterns in place that are about to produce pain. That is what He did for this woman when He notified her that she missed being stoned now, but rocks, humiliation, and shame would fly her way again if she didn't change the lifestyle that is producing those results!"

Jesus understood that if we don't deal with the way we think and the principles we believe, then storms cycle! It will come back around, and around, and around, and around. We act shocked that the depression we fought off five years ago is back. However, we could have forecasted it because we wouldn't address the negative voices in our lives.

> JESUS UNDERSTOOD THAT IF WE DON'T DEAL WITH THE WAY WE THINK AND THE PRINCIPLES WE BELIEVE, THEN STORMS CYCLE!

The forecast is clear . . . marriage trouble is coming because we refuse to do the hard and painful work of changing the attitudes or actions that cause the strife and pain. Even after counseling/retreats/seminars, we march right back to the same climate. The weather may change for a week or two, but the forecast is apparent. The forecast is that you will end up with the wrong person . . . again. How can we be sure? Because you keep going back to the wrong climate to find someone. You keep going to clubs and can't figure out why he isn't the God-fearing, spiritually-minded priest of your home! You frequent the dating bar. Then you can't wrap your mind around why she won't cover up in modesty or want to stay home with you on a Friday night. The climate forecasted what he or she would be! You just didn't like the forecast, so you ignored it!

Jesus forecasts . . . "Woman go and sin no more." Why? Because if you are rescued and go back to sin . . . your lack of a changed climate will result in a repeat performance. Jesus tells the woman caught in adultery to go and sin no more. After raising him from the dead, why didn't He look at Lazarus and say, "Go and sin no more"? After healing the man at the pool, why didn't He say, "Go and sin no more"? He dealt with their storm, but He didn't deal with climate. He knew that the climate of original sin meant that Lazarus was going to die again, and the man at the pool would get sick again (the climate of the fallen world ensures this). However, to the woman, He said go and sin no more because He recognized that she had the opportunity to decide to control the climate and not end up in the same predicament.

Some of us are freaking out about today's weather. The truth we like to ignore and refuse to take responsibility for is that the weather could have been avoided because it was probably forecasted. I am thankful for weather forecasts (when they are correct). They help us plan and avoid interruptions and inconveniences. If we pay attention to pertinent information and analyze available data, we will find an interruption-stopping, danger-avoiding forecast for life. Her track record indicates she will break your heart. It is time for avoidance mode. His business practices reveal he will cost you money. Don't shake his hand; instead, put your hand on your wallet and evade. The car is a lemon. I know the rims are sick, and the paint is spotless, but walk . . . no, run away from the deal. Examine the climate, see the future, listen to forecasters (more about these people in the next chapter), and escape unscathed. Choose to ignore the forecast . . . get ready to be rocked!

# 4. WIND COMES SWEEPING DOWN THE PLAINS

Seventeen miles per hour on average. That is what I was told in grade school. That isn't how fast my car could go or that I could run. Seventeen miles per hour is the average wind speed we experience daily in Oklahoma. The winds truly do come sweeping down the plains! That wind impacts everything! The way we golf (low so that it cuts through), generate electricity (windmill farms dot the landscape of Western Oklahoma), and even our hairstyles. I sported a mullet into the early 1990's! That's right, I didn't bow to cultural pressure! I kept my long, curly mane even when it was no longer "cool" (go ahead, call me a rebel)! However, when we moved back to Oklahoma, we had only been here a couple of months when an appointment with the barber sprinted up my "to-do list." Simply because the wind made it impossible to fight the frizz! It is so windy in Oklahoma that we don't normally make note of windy days but rather highlight the days when there is an absence of wind. We are comfortable with the wind. There is an account in Jesus' life that involves wind. However, unlike Oklahoma life, wind didn't make the headlines or receive much attention. The rest of the story is much too dramatic.

Mark 4:35-40 (MSG)

> *Late that day He said to them, "Let's go across to the other side." They took Him in the boat as he was. Other boats came along. A huge storm came up. Waves poured into the boat, threatening to sink it. And Jesus was in the stern, head on a pillow, sleeping! They roused Him, saying, "Teacher, is it nothing to you that we're going down?"*

*Awake now, He told the wind to pipe down and said to the sea, "Quiet! Settle down!" The wind ran out of breath; the sea became smooth as glass.*

It is a startling account. We have already learned by this time that Jesus can speak to sickness. He has demonstrated power over death by raising the widow's son to life. He has multiplied meager provisions into a buffet. Now, we are reminded that Jesus is like us. He gets tired and needs naps. Thank God we also learn that Jesus gets impatient and frustrated with hardheaded folks who can't seem to get what He has been trying to teach them. We learn that folks who were actually and physically with Jesus on a daily basis struggle with faith at times. In response to their "lack of faith" and paralyzing fear, Jesus flexes His divine muscles and calls a halt to the bad weather. After this incredible moment, it is no wonder we have elevated Jesus to a "weatherman" status. However, after hearing this story in children's church, watching it play out on flannel graphs (yes, I am old enough to have seen those), and taking notes on preachers who have used this as a backdrop to address storms, I am no longer struck by Jesus' ability to stop waves.

IT IS UNDERSTANDABLE THAT WE FIXATE ON THE WAVES IN THIS STORY BECAUSE WE ALL FACE WIPEOUT WAVES!

It is understandable that we fixate on the waves in this story because we all face wipeout waves! High, powerful, boat-sinking, life-altering, unstoppable, stomach-churning, white knuckle, holding on for dear life waves with scary names like "cancer," "bankruptcy," "divorce," and "death." And truthfully, you can understand it when you read the story and ask, "What was about to capsize the boat?" What had this group of experienced sailors ready to retire their sea legs to never again venture from dry land? What was visible? What was frightening? The waves. The white caps would have seemed to be the most pressing issue. Right? So, ignoring the "Do Not Disturb" sign, His bedhead, and His need for a break, the disciples rouse an exhausted Jesus and plead with Him to deal with their waves.

The tendency is to shake our heads at these guys. I mean, come on, guys, you have Jesus on board. He prophesied before you ever got on the boat when He said, "Let's go to the other side!" He left no doubt that you would make it through. However, maybe we should give them some grace and cut them some serious slack because we tend to do the same thing even with Jesus on board our lives. We beg Jesus in every prayer service, every altar call, and every nightly bedtime prayer to deal with our waves. Deal with my debt. Deal with my spouse. Deal with my sickness. Deal with my kids. Deal with my job. Deal with my car. These are the obvious, deadly, peace-pummeling, and serenity-swamping waves that we see pouring into our lives, and we can't seem to help it . . . we panic. Therefore, when we read the account, we wave watch. . . and we miss it.

After reading this passage hundreds of times, if not thousands, the Holy Spirit turned the light on to something I hadn't really paid any attention to in the past. Knowing that Jesus isn't simply a weatherman and that He is determined to change climate, it hit me. Reread it. Jump to verse 39 of the account and read it slowly . . . very slowly and carefully.

He got up, rebuked the wind, and said to the waves, *"Quiet! Be still!"* Then, the wind died down, and it was completely calm.

You missed it, didn't you? I did until I read it while focused on order. The disciples are asking for assistance with their waves. However, Jesus first speaks to the wind. His conversation with the wind is summarized in this statement: "He rebuked the wind." The exact words He said to the wind aren't important, but the order in which He addressed the wind and waves is critical. Why? I believe Jesus knew that waves are dependent on the wind! In other words, He speaks to the wind first because He knew that the climate of wind, unless addressed, would produce more waves. If He didn't stop the wind first, then it was just a matter of time until waves would begin to swell and seasick sailors would be back nervously poking Jesus, trying to wake Him up from His next nap.

In this short conversation with the elements, Jesus gets to the bottom line of most of our issues and problems. He cuts to the chase! He shows us that waves of destruction will keep rolling in until we deal with the wind that is driving those waves! You might as well buckle up. You better man up and make the difficult decisions to speak to the climate. Address the climate. Get to the root of what is causing the wild ride and deal with it. Silence the climate, and the waves will stop.

The truth is that most of us beg, plead, and negotiate deals to try to get Jesus to deal with our waves, but we won't let Him or anyone else address or deal with the winds of our lives. Too many of us have actually grown very comfortable with what is causing us to capsize! Don't get me wrong; we don't like the waves (the fear, the anger, the hurt, the bondage. the struggle), but we are content with what is driving those waves. We don't like the cycle of being hungover on Saturday, but we refuse to stay at home on Friday night. We march right out into the wind! We don't like the wave of having a broken heart, but God help the person who challenges us to address the wind of being physically intimate before we are married. We despise the cycle of being broke. We will beg Jesus and our family members to help us stop the waves. However, let a pastor, a financial advisor, or a good friend try to get us to cut up our credit cards, and we will use the scissors we should have used on the card as a weapon to fight for wind. Waves will not stop until we first address the wind.

The challenge is that to cut off the wind, Jesus usually sends someone into your life who can identify your wind! Yet, we tend to get angry when they won't stop the waves! As a pastor, I see it all of the time. Folks want their bills paid but get angry when someone tries to help them take steps to learn how to handle the money they already have. People grow incredibly comfortable begging for what they need and buying what they want. Waves of debt, collectors calling, but their nails are professionally done, and they have the latest, greatest $600 phone. Folks want their broken heart healed but get angry when you balk at who they are about to go out with or will refuse to quit living with the "windy" person who produces the waves that are so scary. They are comfortable with trying to find a prince/princess in the gutter. Then, wide-eyed, panic-stricken, and confused when they can't fathom why that person wants to go back to the wavy climate they found themselves in originally. Folks want the wave-stopping blessings of Jesus but get angry when you try to convince them that being faithful in attendance, giving, and serving are key components of stopping the wind! People will wake you from (or keep you from) a Sunday nap to weep and bemoan the pain of sin. Then, in the very next breath, they will make excuses and flat-out refuse to stop the very behavior that is breathing momentum into the waves pouring over the rails of their life. Oh, they love Jesus . . . but they refuse to allow Him (or you) to talk to their wind.

Who do you have who can step into your climate and not just speak to storms. . . not just the waves . . . but the wind? You may think you need a wave stopper. What would do us the most good, and what we most need, is a wind stopper. We need someone (a trusted friend, a proven pastor, a counselor) who can look at us and say, "Go and stop this!" and, even if we are comfortable with the wind, . . . we obey! Through the Holy Spirit's power, these folks often see what we can't see. As we listen to them, we discover that miracles almost always reside on the other side of obedience.

You can hide from the wind for a while! You can claim smooth sailing. However, eventually, the waves reveal reality. Rough waters. Bucking boats. Rocky marriages. Choppy credit. Soaked schedules. Winds are present and need to be addressed. Let the Wind Stopper rise up and speak to the wind. The waves will have no choice but to follow . . . even in Oklahoma!

# 5. PORCHES AND PIGS

A crowd gathered. Ears tuned to the sound of His voice. With a verbal paintbrush, a story complex in plot and rich in truth is constructed. Spontaneously and with supernatural skill, He crafts a tale that will cause the likes of Charles Dickens and William Shakespeare to shake their head in awe. For centuries to come, the account will be fodder for poems, ballets, and even paintings by the likes of Rembrandt. But, perhaps it is best to view the story through a "Norman Rockwell" filter. I wish you could read with your eyes closed so that you could recreate the scene in your mind.

Peering down the hillside, you see the homestead. Surrounded by a strong split rail fence. The yard is expansive. The long winding drive cuts down the left side of the property. Cast off toys, long forgotten, litter the yard, and remind you that time has passed quickly. The house is impressive and has two stories. Large, but not overwhelming. Black shutters flank each window. Landscaping manicured and yard trimmed. In the background, barns are well-kept. Swarming activity can be seen as the investment of hard days in the fields that must now be managed. Affluent, but not flashy. Wealthy, but not wasteful. There are prominent features, such as the windmill, the corrals, and the worn tire swing under the aged tree that stands towering alone in the front yard. However, the one feature that stands out above all else is the large, inviting, wraparound porch lined with rocking chairs. A small round table holds the oft-used checkers set. A sleeping dog is stationed near the screen door. Muddy boots from the field are left on the first step. It is a gathering place at the end of a long day of planting or harvest. Iced tea and lemonade have been shared here, as well as late-night cups of hot chocolate in the cool fall evenings. Dates end in the swing on the far end of the porch, where long moments of silence are filled with spectacular views of the star-filled sky. The porch has served as "base" during intense games of tag. It has served as a retreat from sudden spring showers. Here, stories, jokes, and serious discussions have found an audience. Laughs, tears, and life have been experienced on this porch.

Jesus uses this scene to craft His masterpiece that we now call "The Parable of The Prodigal Son" in Luke 15:11-31.

Jesus sketches this time-tested story but leaves out some key information. For instance, we are not given explanations or reasons. But, honestly, would the details matter? Would it help us to know that the cause was rebellion, immaturity, the need for adventure, or the culmination of an argument? The result, the outcome is the same . . . the youngest son exits the scene. He grabs the old duffle bag, empties out his dresser drawers, and stomps down the stairs, determined to make it on his own. He leaves his mother shattered in tears. He finds his father in the study going over herd counts, demands an early inheritance (basically saying he wished his dad was dead), opens the screen door as his father sits stunned, confused, scared, and scarred, and, without hesitation or a second thought, steps off the porch and heads into a new life. Naive? Stupid? Tricked? Duped? Dumb? Again, the reason, or reasoning, doesn't change the reality of a son gone. The news didn't go exactly like the son had imagined. With the soundtrack of "I Did It My Way" playing in his mind, he has visions of easy street, freedom from rules and curfews, friends, fun, and true love as his intended end. Swanky restaurants give way to swine slop. Posh hotels are traded for pig pens. "Friends" vanish as quickly as his fortune. Famine finalizes his fall.

We can't imagine this plummet. How did he end up like this? He had more than enough. He had comfort. He was set up for success. The fall is too dramatic and too far. It makes no sense. But to understand how he winds up so far gone, you must go back and realize that the final step into the pig pen took place when he took the first step off the porch. In fact, when you consider the story again, instead of asking all of the "why" questions, perhaps the best question to ask is simply "What?" Rather than why he did this or fell so fast, the more important question is what changed? What led to his demise?" What caused a rich and favored young man to end up face down in a mud hole with pigs as company? And not only what caused his fall, but what changed when he came to his senses? How did he correct his mistake? How did he go from outcast to son again? Ironically, the same thing that messed everything up was the same thing that resolved the situation. When he stepped off the porch, he changed the climate. When he finally comes to his senses (maybe a better way to say it is when he grows up) and starts home, after wasting everything, and enters the front yard, he simply changes climate. He overlooks and undervalues climate, and disaster ensues. He corrects the climate, and the weather changes in his favor. Climate change put him back on the porch and, subsequently, back under protection and provision. The great truth and hope this account teaches us is that there is a way to turn things around. We simply change the climate, and everything else changes.

> THE GREAT TRUTH AND HOPE THIS ACCOUNT TEACHES US IS THAT THERE IS A WAY TO TURN THINGS AROUND.

My grandmother was terribly afraid of storms. At the first sign of a dark cloud or a less-than-favorable weather update, she would stick her head out of the screen door and yell at my sister and me to get back in the house. I hated to stop playing, but she would insist because she knew that safety was ensured by being back in the right climate. Safety could be found on the porch! The lightning couldn't get us there. The hail might damage the roof, but it wouldn't hit our heads. The porch was lifesaving and safe living.

Most of us who are suffering in the pig pens of life simply need to get back on the porch. But how? What steps do we need to take to get back home? How do we leave the climate we have created, and in some cases, demanded and fought for, to find a new and safe climate? There is a rocking chair on the porch. Sit down. It will take several cups of cocoa or coffee to consider the characteristics which Paul shares that are necessary to establish "Kingdom Climate" in our life. But no worries . . . you are safe on the porch . . . now we just have to fight to stay here.

# 6. THE REST OF THE STORY

It could only be found on an AM Station. I know, I know. You probably don't even know what an AM station is. Car makers have even talked about no longer including AM stations on the radios of their new cars. But back in the day, you could dial into these low-powered stations for local shows and news. Once a day, just after the noon news report, the deep, rich, and distinguishable voice would cut through the ever-present static and begin telling a story I usually thought I knew. However, there was always a back story with which I wasn't really familiar. This new part of the story would add an unexpected twist and turn and, ultimately, lead to an "ah ha" moment. Paul Harvey, with the perfect pause for effect, would end these tales with the now famous statement . . . "Now you know the rest of the story."

We know the familiar part of the following passage in Romans. We learn it early. It is a key text in the rite of passage for most Christian youth. You quote it. The youth leaders quote it. Pastors thump on pulpits while referencing it. T-shirts are emblazoned with it. The known part of the story is trapped in the confines of the eloquent but lengthy and sometimes rambling thoughts of Paul. Perhaps we have cherry-picked it because of its quotability. However, until we push past the two familiar verses, we miss not only the rest of the story but also the climate-changing instructions. You know the passage . . . make your parents, youth pastor, and pastor quote it with you!

Romans 12:1-2 (NIV)

> *Therefore, I urge you, brothers and sisters, in view of God's mercy, to offer your bodies as a living sacrifice, holy and pleasing to God—this is your true and proper worship. Do not conform to the pattern of this world, but be transformed by the renewing of your mind. Then you will be able to test and approve what God's will is—his good, pleasing and perfect will.*

Paul begins by challenging us to "renew" our minds. He knew we come out of bad climate into Kingdom Climate head first. Another way to say this is that we must change the way we think. As one pastor said, "You will come out of every problem head first!" Scripture is correct. As a man thinks, so is he! Climate is indeed, in large part, dictated by how we think. The fact is, once we encounter Jesus, our soul is saved, but our mind is often still lost and controlled by principalities! Principalities govern by setting up guidelines or truths (principles) that we must unlearn. That is the first and necessary step to accomplishing climate change is to realize that when we come into relationship with Christ we, according to Paul in 1 Corinthians 2:16, "have the mind of Christ." So, to change our minds, we must learn to think like Christ.

This idea of having the mind of Christ assures us that Jesus was on a mission to do more than just save our souls! He also wants to redeem/reconcile/restore everything that was lost in man's fall, and in the fall, we lost more than just relationship, dominion, and authority! We lost our mind. This is why Jesus addresses more than just our hearts and souls in Matthew 22:37 (NIV): *"Love the Lord your God with all your heart and with all your soul and with all your mind."*

Jesus knew we are made up of three parts . . . heart (flesh), soul (spirit), and mind. Man's "mind" is an organ of the soul and is his computer by which he stores information gained through his six senses. The mind, like the heart, is a separate but integral part of the soul. Paul tries to explain how all of this works. He says in Galatians 5:17 (NLT), *"For the flesh lusts against the Spirit, and the Spirit against the flesh: and these are contrary the one to the other: so that you cannot do the things that you would."* Then, in Romans 8:7 (NKJV), *"Because the carnal mind is enmity against God: for it is not subject to the law of God, neither indeed can be."* Paul is teaching us that there is a war going on inside of us. The spiritual part of us is at war against the mind that has been established in us. Dharius Daniels calls this "The Reality of Duality!"

Then Paul comes along in Romans 7:25 (MEV) and lets us in on a truth that makes victory possible. *"I thank God **through Jesus Christ our Lord**. So then, with my mind, I serve the law of God, but with my flesh, the law of sin."* Paul contends that "through Jesus," we are able to serve God with our minds! What determines if I serve God? My flesh doesn't. My spirit, now under submission to the Holy Spirit, must be allowed to overtake my carnal mind. Another way to say this is that my flesh doesn't determine where my life goes. My mind, being ruled by the Holy Spirit, determines where my life goes. My soul wants to delight in the Lord, but my carnal mind is warring against my soul/spirit. So, where your mind goes, your life goes. Paul, correctly, starts with our mind. Let me be absolutely clear: I (and neither is Paul) am not talking about willpower. If you could do this with willpower, then you would not need Jesus! I am talking about learning to allow the spirit to override our minds. We retrain our brain by reading His Words and examining closely how He "thought" through moments in His life. Jesus is our role and thought model. However, we don't stop there. We also change our thought patterns through the books we read, the people we listen to (this is also why it is so important to have a Bible-preaching preacher!), and by examining the lives of godly folks who are living like we want to live. These people model marriage, managing money, and navigating relationships for us; we must learn how they think! They are literal and living examples of the climate we are trying to establish. We can't overlook these steps!

> MY SPIRIT, NOW UNDER SUBMISSION TO THE HOLY SPIRIT, MUST BE ALLOWED TO OVERTAKE MY CARNAL MIND.

However, changing our mindset is just the initial step. Too often, we only address our mind, but we never practically walk out the change that we are trying to embrace in our head. Yes, our mind has to change, but so must our actions and how we live. We must move past the quotability of the first two verses of Romans 12 and wrestle with the rest of the chapter. It is apparent that Paul believed that a mind change was supposed to start the process of climate change. However, he must have also believed that there should be distinct and very evident characteristics that are set into motion by the mind change. He implores us to change our thoughts and then lists the next steps. He gives us seventeen characteristics of the Kingdom Climate that provide a structure for lasting, permanent change. So, we can't afford to stop at verse two. It is only as we push deeper that we discover that Paul literally maps out the characteristics (principles, governing guidelines, truths) that must be established to create a Kingdom Climate so that we also get Kingdom Weather.

This is where we must slow down and do the hardest work. A close examination and implementation, through the power of the Spirit, of these characteristics is what will produce a climate change that forces the weather to change forever! I encourage you to pause here before continuing. Climate change will not take place uncontested. The easy part, recognizing the need for change, is over. To actually create or effect change, you will have to take one chapter at a time, work it out, and once that characteristic is established in your life, then and only then move on to the next. Don't get me wrong; as you make changes, you will not only begin to see changes in the weather of your life, but an entire change of climate. It is a grueling but worthwhile journey.

Stop and read the entirety of the verses that follow, and then we will break them down, climate-changing characteristic by climate-changing characteristic.

Romans 12:3-21 (NIV)

> *For by the grace given me I say to every one of you: Do not think of yourself more highly than you ought, but rather think of yourself with sober judgment, in accordance with the faith God has distributed to each of you. For just as each of us has one body with many members, and these members do not all have the same function, so in Christ we, though many, form one body, and each member belongs to all the others. We have different gifts, according to the grace given to each of us. If your gift is prophesying, then prophesy in accordance with your faith; if it is serving, then serve; if it is teaching, then teach; if it is to encourage, then give encouragement; if it is giving, then give generously; if it is to lead, do it diligently; if it is to show mercy, do it cheerfully. Love must be sincere. Hate what is evil; cling to what is good. Be devoted to one another in love. Honor one another above*

*yourselves. Never be lacking in zeal, but keep your spiritual fervor, serving the Lord. Be joyful in hope, patient in affliction, faithful in prayer. Share with the Lord's people who are in need. Practice hospitality. Bless those who persecute you; bless and do not curse. Rejoice with those who rejoice; mourn with those who mourn. Live in harmony with one another. Do not be proud, but be willing to associate with people of low position. Do not be conceited. Do not repay anyone evil for evil. Be careful to do what is right in the eyes of everyone. If it is possible, as far as it depends on you, live at peace with everyone. Do not take revenge, my dear friends, but leave room for God's wrath, for it is written: "It is mine to avenge; I will repay," says the Lord. On the contrary: "If your enemy is hungry, feed him; if he is thirsty, give him something to drink. In doing this, you will heap burning coals on his head." Do not be overcome by evil, but overcome evil with good.*

These often passed-over, overlooked, and simply ignored verses are probably not as memorable or quotable. They certainly don't fit well on shirts or bumper stickers. However, it is this "rest of the story" that we must examine in order to find true climate change.

# 7. CONNECT FOUR (ACTUALLY MORE)

**Kingdom Climate Characteristic 1: Connect**

Did you play the game when you were a kid? The goal was to get four checkers in a row. It didn't matter if it was a vertical line or horizontal. Straight up or down or diagonal. Victory was the result of simply aligning four connected checkers. However, if you played this game, then you also know that it wasn't as simple as it sounds. The challenge was that your opponent was also attempting to connect four checkers. In their efforts to get their pieces lined up, they would inevitably interrupt our run. Worse was that your opponent would sometimes even intentionally use their pieces to block your row to keep you from being connected. They did this because they knew what Paul knew . . . connecting results in a win. Paul knew that a change to Kingdom Climate would originate in, and with, connection.

Romans 12:4-6 (NIV)

> *For just as each of us has one body with many members, and these members do not all have the same function, so in Christ we, though many, form one body, and each member belongs to all the others. We have different gifts, according to the grace given to each of us. If your gift is prophesying, then prophesy in accordance with your faith.*

Our ability to win is attached to our ability to be connected. Unfortunately, our opponent also understands this strategy, so he often interrupts. He does this with to-do lists, events, and with life. Our "run" to connection is stymied by so many other "important" and "necessary" things. In fact, this enemy is so committed to keeping us from connection that he will block connection by whatever means necessary. He will use offense, pettiness, busyness, distractions, promotions, sickness, or anything else he can to keep us isolated and defeated. The result is that we face storm clouds alone and exposed.

Reread verses 4-6 in the Message Bible.

> *Each part gets its meaning from the body as a whole, not the other way around. The body we're talking about is Christ's body of chosen people. Each of us finds our meaning and function as a part of his body. But as a chopped-off finger or cut-off toe we wouldn't amount to much, would we?*

Kingdom Climate is established in connectedness. Paul tells us that when our mind is transformed, Kingdom Climate will be established, which in turn will impact the weather of our life. For this to happen, we must be connected to the body! Why? Paul knew that the climate of isolation produces the weather of loneliness, paranoia, and suspicion and makes us vulnerable to the accusations and temptations of the enemy. We are incomplete apart from being in the body. Our connectedness is our life source.

We tend to think that being told we need to be connected to a local body is simply a rouse by which the local pastor is just trying to build his attendance. However, this is about climate! Who you are connected to will dictate climate, which will then dictate weather. Many of us are more connected to our office mates than to the body members! By the way, this goes beyond just attendance. You are not connected just because you attend a church. Attendance is first base and beginner level in connection. **Some of us never reap climate change because we only sow attendance.** If we want the full fruit of connectedness, we must become involved in each other's lives. Serve together. Sit together. Share life together.

The Lone Ranger was one of my favorite shows as a kid. It was probably because of my affinity for guns and horses. I can still remember watching in awe as the masked hero would ride into trouble week after week and always come out victorious and unscathed. What I failed to realize as a kid was that The Lone Ranger really wasn't that "Lone!" He had a partner. A confidant. A person he could count on and to whom he was connected. Tonto! Tonto wasn't the star, but he was essential to the star's success. For some reason, we fixate on the Lone Ranger and forget that, without Tonto, the Lone Ranger would have been killed in the very first week. Undoubtedly, The Lone Ranger was a great TV show, but it is a horrible model for the Kingdom Climate.

We were never intended to travel this road by ourselves. Together, we are a formidable foe. Isolated, we are an easy target. We must be connected. Then, we move even deeper into the covenant so that we can anticipate and expect the body to function according to its intended design. The reason we see the body fail to function properly is because parts are out of alignment or are not fulfilling their function. So, to function properly, we must be so tuned into one another that we carry and comfort each other. Jesus knew that by themselves, the disciples would be destroyed! So, Jesus sent His followers out and into the world two by two rather than one by one.

> TOGETHER, WE ARE A FORMIDABLE FOE. ISOLATED, WE ARE AN EASY TARGET.

In their book *Fearfully and Wonderfully Made*, Paul Bland and Phillip Yancy quote a physician who said, "A cell can live separately in the body." This doctor went on to say, "In fact, some cells choose to live inside the body, sharing its benefits while maintaining complete independence. The two medical names these separate cells are given: either parasites or cancer." No one would say they want to have a parasite or a cancer in their physical body. However, when we don't really connect, we fall into one of those two categories. We are either sucking and stealing life from others, or we are eating away at the very function of the body."

Too many of us come to the conclusion that it would be easier if we could live life isolated. Isolation would surely insulate us and inoculate us against pain. We convince, or perhaps, a more accurate word would be deceive ourselves into living as if we don't need relationship. However, one of the earliest truths that we discover in the Bible is found in Genesis Two. When on the sixth day of creation, after stating that everything He has crafted and designed up to this point is "good," God creates man, and, for the first time, He sees His handiwork and declares, "It isn't good!" This isn't a reflection on His creation but the state of His creation. Does He state that it isn't good for man to be clothed? Feathered? Rich? Wealthy? Famous? Happy? No . . . He says it isn't good for man to be ALONE! Isolation is not God's design or plan for man. In fact, we quickly figure out that man cannot fulfill his God-given assignment by himself.

**In Psalms 68:6, we are told that God's stated plan is to place the isolated in families.** However, I run into many offended Christians who have quit church after church simply because they have been hurt by church folks! Everyone I run into seems to be mad at someone . . . church family, immediate family, coworkers, etc. There are so many people who faithfully sit in services weekly, who are in bondage because they are in a war that wasn't civil. Simply put, there are just way too many of us walking wounded and offended and subsequently disconnected. What good does it do if God places us in a family and brings us out of isolation if we fight our way back into isolation?

**Your connectedness determines your strength.** It determines your effectiveness. We have bought the lie that being in a room once a week, staring at the back of each other's heads, and maybe greeting one another at the instruction of the pastor equals connected and will suffice. Our society assigns friendship to a surface-level connection that really reveals no genuine relationship (just look at Facebook). Some of us go all week with no connection. Then, when a preacher talks about being connected, our initial response/thought/excuse is, "Well, nobody checked on me!" Here is the climate change . . . Who have you checked on? What you sow, you reap! You have to sow a climate of connectedness to reap connectedness.

It is important to note in a discussion about connection that **intimacy is incremental.** Paul isn't calling us to simply claim connection after one meeting. He isn't instructing us to meet someone on Facebook or once at a bookstore and tell them our entire life story. Too often, we give them our business, and they haven't earned that level of access. Time allows us to incrementally trust - to share the intimate. **Kingdom Climate dictates connectedness, but that connectedness must also be vetted.**

Jesus called men to be with Him (Mark 3:14) so that He could have both relationship and fellowship. He knew that being connected was paramount! **He knew that those who are close matter most! People create climate.** So, if climate is what causes change and controls the direction of our lives, then we must manage our relationships to manage the trajectory of our lives! Our destiny is determined not just by who we are, but it is also equally affected by where we are and who we are with. We should know that relationships are important because, in the garden, the devil was idle until God put Eve in it. **It wasn't until relationship was established that the enemy went on the offensive.** So, relationships are paramount.

Proverbs 17:17 (NIV) states that *"A friend loves at all times, and a brother is born for a time of adversity."*

Solomon was trying to tell us that Kingdom Climate relationships are **assigned to your life for the tough times.** God positions people for us! We generally assign the greatest level of friendship to those with whom we laugh, vacation, and have fun. **However, a climate-changing relationship is there for the tough times. In fact, the wise man said they were born for that.**

Think about this incredibly profound thought! God brought them into existence for your hard time! Think about the process that involved . . . man and woman born, brought together, date, break up, date, engaged, cold feet, married, have a baby, baby grows up, ends up in the same geographic location as you all so that they are on-site for your tear-filled moments. Desire to see miracles? Stop looking past the people who have been dependable in your heart-breaking moments. Quit sending folks away who are there to help your real story become a healthy story! We have confused relationships of convenience with those that are covenant. Therefore, what happens is we avoid or abandon covenant relationships for convenient relationships, which we can enter and exit at will with no accountability or responsibility. Then we get confused and sometimes even angry when we expect to reap the fruit of covenant relationships when we haven't paid the high cost of covenant. Covenant is expensive. It costs tears, sacrifice, and being willing to fight for someone who can never pay you back or promote you.

> WE HAVE CONFUSED RELATIONSHIPS OF CONVENIENCE WITH THOSE THAT ARE COVENANT.

**Pain proves relationship! When your life is at its worst, your friends have to be at their best.** If they are true friends, they won't summarize your success and write a chapter on your failure. They won't let what you did in one chapter taint the entire book. They will be trustworthy to handle your business even when your business is a mess! Who do you have in your life that is reliable during adversity? If everyone around you backpedals and runs when it gets tough, then they are not friends! If you run for the hills when your "friend" is struggling and their situation is overwhelming, then let's be honest; you are not a friend! Climate change begins with connection! In fact, when we are not connected, look at the progression that takes place. Jesus' disciples ask for the signs that will show them that the end is coming. Here is His response in Matthew 24:3-13 (KJV):

> *And as he sat upon the mount of Olives, the disciples came unto him privately, saying, Tell us, when shall these things be? and what shall be the sign of thy coming, and of the end of the world? And Jesus answered and said unto them, "Take heed that no man deceive you. For many shall come in my name, saying, I am Christ; and shall deceive many. And ye shall hear of wars and rumors of wars: see that ye be not troubled: for all these things must come to pass, but the end is not yet. For nation shall rise against nation, and kingdom against kingdom: and there shall be famines, and pestilences, and earthquakes, in divers places. All these are the beginning of sorrows. Then shall they deliver you up to be afflicted, and shall kill you: and ye shall be hated of all nations for my name's sake. And then shall many be offended, and shall betray one another, and shall hate one another. And many false prophets shall rise, and shall deceive many. And because iniquity shall abound, the love of many shall wax cold. But he that shall endure unto the end, the same shall be saved.*

Right in the middle of this horrid list that would indicate we are in the last days, Jesus pauses and says all this bad stuff - wars, famines, earthquakes - **is just the beginning of sorrows**. What? You mean it is going to get worse from here? I didn't think it could get any worse. That is some pretty nasty weather already. So how could it get worse, Jesus? He lists the list of the worse weather, and leading the parade is that many will be offended. Believers will betray one another, hate one another, and then they are deceived and, ultimately, lose their love for Christ and fall away.

Watch the progression Jesus shares. Offense leads to betrayal. Because if you offended me, I no longer feel the need to carry your burden. I no longer feel the need to protect you. I no longer feel the need to keep your business your business. When I am offended, I will say things I wouldn't say otherwise. I will share things I wouldn't share otherwise. Then betrayal leads to hate. I was offended, but now I can't even stand to see you. I don't want to be around you. I will duck to another aisle at the grocery store. I will wait in the car in the parking lot until I know you have cleared the lobby, and then I will enter. I will leave church service before you so that I don't have to talk or make eye contact. I can't say your name without the snarl at the end of it.

John Bevere says, "Offenses of the heart that are not dealt with end up leading to betrayal, and betrayals not dealt with end up in hatred."

Hate leads to becoming vulnerable to deception. We reason, "If they said they loved me, but they offended me so badly, then their word must not be true. If their word isn't true, then the ONE they represent must be a liar too. If God's people are going to act like that, then why would I want to be one of them? Surely, if one is like that, then they are all like that." This deception can lead to falling away or walking away from Christ.

**Jesus makes the argument that connection is what will be attacked in the last days.** In doing so, He emphasizes that it is connection which is so vitally important to our ability to endure to the end. He declares that one of the worst things that can happen to us is relationships being broken. So, I can safely make this logical jump . . . **If I fall out of love with God's people, then ultimately, I fall out of love with God.** Could it be we fall out of love with Christ when we fall out of love with one another? Could it be that our love for Jesus wains when our love for one another wains? According to Jesus, you can't separate the two.

My wife and I have concluded that church people today don't seem to want to do as much together. Maybe it is because we have started down the progression, fallen for the trap, and our anger has led us to fall away! Maybe our love for God is waxing cold because we don't love the people we are on the path with. Maybe our worship is dry and lifeless because when we walk in the door, we are loveless towards the people we are worshipping with. Maybe the reason we spend less time at church is that the offense has opened the door for us to believe we don't need time with each other. Maybe our lack of connection with God is a direct result of our lack of connection with God's people!

If we are going to establish Kingdom Climate, then we cannot do so without first addressing our need for kingdom connection. We need brothers and sisters in Christ to help us identify, evade, and change climates that would produce the weather we hope to avoid. Some of us are facing weather that we would not face if we were connected! However, because we are all by ourselves, we are swamped! **Christianity has not and never will be for "Lone Rangers!"**

The weather that many of us face would be survived easily if we were connected. However, too many of us have saddled up a white horse, thrown on a mask, and repeatedly tried to ride into storms only to be swamped! Are you connected to a friend? Are you connected to a group? Are you connected to a body? Who is your Tonto? Who can you call in the middle of the night? Who can you turn to in the middle of a storm? But this is a two-way street. Whose Tonto are you, Kemosabe (which means "trusty scout" or "faithful friend")?

# 8. IN IT TO WIN IT!

**Kingdom Climate Characteristic 2: Serve**

Paul implores us to connect to the body. It is our lifeline. However, in our society, we like to think that we are more connected than we have ever been. Thousands of friends are as "close" as the push of a button. Instant and constant connection. Second by second, play-by-play of every aspect of their life, from what they are eating at the moment to what they are listening to on their headphones. We are connected . . . aren't we? How do we know if we are really connected? Are we connected just because we attend? If I show up a certain number of times each month in a scheduled service, then surely that reveals and proves that I am connected, doesn't it? At least, that seems to be what we have convinced ourselves. But showing up isn't really enough. In fact, Paul stops long enough to give us a litmus test to reveal just how connected we are. See if you can spot the test found in Romans 12:4-7 (NIV).

> *For just as each of us has one body with many members, and these members do not all have the same function, so in Christ we, though many, form one body, and each member belongs to all the others. We have different gifts, according to the grace given to each of us. If your gift is prophesying, then prophesy in accordance with your faith; if it is serving, then serve; if it is teaching, then teach; if it is to encourage, then give encouragement; if it is giving, then give generously; if it is to lead, do it diligently; if it is to show mercy, do it cheerfully.*

**Paul makes it clear that not only is the second characteristic of Kingdom Climate our willingness to serve,** but he also says our level of connectedness is shown by whether we serve. In fact, Paul seems more interested in the climate of kingdom service than he is in the gift that is being used to serve. So, it doesn't matter if it is teaching, encouraging, giving, leading, or showing mercy. Paul says we should serve with our gift. As we do, the climate of service will change our weather.

This stands in direct contrast to the climate of most of our lives. **We show up as consumers, and the question we almost always ask reveals the climate we have established. "What can you do for me?"** And if you can't do for me, then I'm out. But Paul says that Kingdom Climate isn't about me or about getting mine. In fact, he proposes that as I give (serve) and others get what they need, I no longer have to worry about my needs being met. I don't have to manipulate or pull strings because what I make happen for others, God makes happen for me. God becomes responsible for what I need so that I can serve freely.

## HAVE YOU EVER NOTICED THAT THE ONE WHO PREPARES A MEAL IS RARELY THE ONE WHO COMPLAINS ABOUT THE FOOD?

Have you ever noticed that the one who prepares a meal is rarely the one who complains about the food? I mean, when you have worked tirelessly for hours mixing, measuring, seasoning, and baking the main course, you don't normally bite into it and begin to degrade its texture or taste. It is those who only show up to consume and have no investment in the process required to prepare the food who want to complain! I believe this is how we know we are connected and serving at the Kingdom Climate level. We are so invested that we don't complain. Instead, we savor every bite (service moment).

The perfect example of what I am talking about is Americans' approach to sports. We pay unconscionable' salaries to people to play games at high levels so that we can claim victory from their sacrifice and hard work. We have developed such an aversion to practice that what we want to do now is skip all the hard work and become experts from the stands. Haven't you met someone who has never taken a snap, never thrown a pass, never studied a playbook, but they sit in a recliner and become an armchair quarterback? That even happens outside the confines of sports, doesn't it? This person has never balanced a budget, made major decisions that affected other people's livelihood, set policy, or hired/fired; and yet, from the water cooler, they have all the answers. This has led us to a proverbial "we." When the guys or girls who put in all the hard work, day after day, take the field and all the practice pays off and they come out on top . . . we say, "we won." Or if they came up short on game day, we duck our heads because "we lost!" When the truth is "we" didn't really do anything. The reality is that it was the people on the field, in the driver's seat, in the big chair sitting at the big desk who won, lost, triumphed, or came up short. We are in the stands but convinced we are in the game.

I have observed some things about the stands.

**In the stands, you can critique.**

My youngest son, Devin, played baseball. I am an avid baseball fan. It was my first love. As Devin progressed through high school, I would go to every game. I would usually position myself directly behind the screen at home plate. When Devin would step to the plate, I would get so aggravated at the home plate umpire when he would call what I knew was a ball a strike. I would grow equally frustrated when Devin would pitch, and the ump would call what was an obvious strike a ball. Ultimately, for Devin's sanity and to keep me from being thrown out of the ballpark as I grew increasingly vocal, I moved to the safety of the press box. Then something interesting happened to me. A friend of mine called and invited me to begin umpiring at the local Little League field. I wanted to stay connected to the game and spend some time with my friend, so I went out, bought all the gear, and showed up at the park, ready to work my first game. I suddenly discovered that calling balls and strikes is much, much easier from behind the screen while you are sitting in a comfortable lawn chair. Suited up as the ump? Well, that is an entirely different matter. Your view is blocked by a face mask and a catcher that seems to constantly be moving and in your way. The same ball that you know the exact location of from the lawn chair is now hurling towards you at 70mph plus and is moving side to side and up and down.

From the stands, I never missed a call. However, in the game, I learned that calling balls and strikes is actually quite difficult. Why do you think players get so upset at reporters when the reporters seem to have all the answers? Why do you think players get angry when they hear an analyst criticize one of their teammates? The player gets angry because they know the outsider doesn't see all the effort, time, study, and strategy that has gone into the game plan. It is easy to snicker from the stands. It is accepted (especially in this day) to make judgments from the cheap seats. The distance from the stands to the field causes us to feel safe to critique. **We can be cruel from the crowd.** Devin, now in college, is still playing baseball. However, I am much quieter at his games than I used to be. I learned my lesson: it is easier to critique from the stands. Your perspective changes when you actually get on the field.

### In the stands, you can root with no risk.

We want our team to give every ounce of energy and hold nothing back. We demand every ounce of effort. We want them in the weight room. We want them to watch their diet (while we are holding popcorn and sugar water in our hands.) We don't want them to ever take a day off. Never let down. Work. Prepare. Stay focused. But those who root have no requirements. We just want to walk in on game day. We forget about the game until the next one. We don't have to prepare. We don't have to focus. We don't have to plan. We just want the game to be good when we get there. I want the worship team on key. I want the preacher holy. I want the greeters friendly. I want the Kids Team in place and creative. I want the sound right and the temperature perfect. I want the length of the service timed out to the second. But I want it that way with no personal investment or effort.

### In the stands, you don't really win!

The stands are safe. The stands are easy. The stands are optional . . . you can show up late and leave early or not show up at all. However, in the stands, although you may experience excitement, you will never experience a win. Not really! You don't get the trophy. You don't get the invitation to the White House. You don't get the parade. You don't get the ring. You don't get your jersey hung in the rafters. You don't get the bonus. Fear keeps many of us out of the game. We are afraid of the criticism or the risk. Maybe we are afraid to get in the game because we have experienced failure in the past. So, we sit in the stands, and we never get to experience the win. We have even done this to church. We have turned church into a spectator sport. I show up and watch you sing for me, you preach at me, you charge me a little entry fee, and then I go home. If church was good or if you hear a story of someone in the crowd who had an incredible experience, then you can say, "We won." But the truth is your life hasn't been changed. Your sickness hasn't been healed. Your family hasn't been transformed. Why? You aren't winning until you personally get in the game yourself. **The fruit of winning comes from the seed that is planted behind the scenes.**

## TO WIN . . . YOU GOT TO GET IN!

How do you think Paul came to the conclusion that service was a key component of Kingdom Climate? He learned it from Jesus. Jesus refused to let people stay on the sidelines. He had a tendency wherever He went (and He still does this today) to force people to make a decision - "take up your cross, let the dead bury the dead, leave your nets, follow me, step out of the boat." He was a pro at forcing people to fold their lawn chairs, gear up, and get in the game! Perhaps one of the greatest examples of this is found in Luke 19:1-10 (TLB).

> *As Jesus was passing through Jericho, a man named Zacchaeus, one of the most influential Jews in the Roman tax-collecting business (and, of course, a very rich man), tried to get a look at Jesus, but he was too short to see over the crowds. So, he ran ahead and climbed into a Sycamore Tree beside the road, to watch from there. When Jesus came by, he looked up at Zacchaeus and called him by name! "Zacchaeus!" he said. "Quick! Come down! For I am going to be a guest in your home today!" Zacchaeus hurriedly climbed down and took Jesus to his house in great excitement and joy. But the crowds were displeased. "He has gone to be the guest of a notorious sinner," they grumbled. Meanwhile, Zacchaeus stood before the Lord and said, "Sir, from now on I will give half my wealth to the poor, and if I find I have overcharged anyone on his taxes, I will penalize myself by giving him back four times as much!" Jesus told him, "This shows that salvation has come to this home today. This man was one of the lost sons of Abraham, and I, the Messiah, have come to search for and to save such souls as his.*

There is no indication that old Zach wanted in the game. He simply wanted to attend on a Sunday to see. His only plan was to hug a tree and hang out on the fringe. **He was expecting to gain perspective, but there is no indication that he planned on participation.** Just get a good seat and watch. Experience the overflow. Experience the excitement of the crowd. But no personal involvement or investment. See, but don't serve!

Jesus found a man in the stands and asked him to get in the game. Notice what happens. People from the stands critique. In the tree, he was safe from the snarky remarks. But now that he has been invited to get in the game, something changes in Zach and to Zach. Once in the game, he becomes a target for sarcasm. You are going to let him serve? Don't you know who he is? Don't you know about his past? Man, if they knew where you were Friday night. So, if you are going to get in the game, then you better get some tough skin . . . apparently, Zach was so focused on the call of Jesus and the fact that Jesus wanted to go to his house that the remarks didn't bother him. **You know if you are really in the game for the right reasons when what other people say doesn't bother or stop you!** The truth is getting in the game is risky. However, Zach determined that having access to Jesus was worth the cost.

We can tell you are serving for the right reasons when the cost never really concerns you. Have you ever met one of those who serve but are martyrs about it? You begin to wonder if they hate it so much, then why are they even doing it? This is why Paul concludes his teaching on the Kingdom Climate of serving by saying to serve with joy. Cheerfully. In other words, if Jesus' yoke is easy and light, you should serve gladly and with a spirit of joy. Paul was trying to get us to ump with a joyful attitude! To greet with a smile on your face. To "ush" cheerfully. Every role should be marked with joy. The worship team should worship cheerfully. It is wrong that Walmart and Chick-fil-A seem to have environments that seem to be more cheerful greeters than some communities of faith. Why should our community and climate be filled with such joy-filled service? It is as you serve that you truly see Jesus!

No more tree-huggers! Climb down. Climb in. Serve! Otherwise, I may just have to call you ... Ooooouuuutttt (said in my best little league umpire voice, complete with the dramatic fist punch in the air!)

# 9. WHAT'S LOVE GOT TO DO WITH IT?

**Kingdom Climate Characteristic 3: Love Sincerely**

If you are an 80s child, then you can't help yourself, can you? You read the title, and you started singing it in your head. It was one of the original earworms. Tina Turner would take the stage, attack the microphone, and with her big hair, loud voice, and louder outfits, she would belt out the question, "What's love got to do with it?" Then she would sing the next line, which posed a follow-up question that should stop us from humming and make us question whether this is a song we agree with at all. In line two of the song, she sung, "What's love but a secondhand emotion?" Really? Love isn't important or crucial? It is just a secondary thing? A minor instead of a major? Leftovers? Her 80s mega-hit certainly stands in direct opposition to what Paul says in Romans 12:9.

Romans 12:9 (NIV) says, *"Love must be sincere. Hate what is evil; cling to what is good."*

The Message Bible says, *"Love from the center of who you are; don't fake it. Run for dear life from evil; hold on for dear life to good."*

Paul addresses sincere love as the third characteristic of Kingdom Climate. However, don't let the order in the list fool you or make you think that maybe Tina was right about it being unimportant. He recognizes it as the crucial component that bears out what the other New Testament writers espoused. Out of the fifty-nine "one another" statements recorded in the New Testaments (identified by Carl F. George, Prepare Your Church for the Future), on seventeen different and distinct occasions, the command is given to love another. Twenty-eight percent of the list is a mandate to love one another. Love is the core component around which all the other commands orbit. Paul stops and says we must love sincerely, knowing that without sincere love, the characteristics that will follow are absolutely impossible to actually experience.

According to folk history, the English word "sincere" comes from two Latin words: sine (without) and cera (wax). In the ancient world, dishonest merchants would use wax to hide defects, such as cracks, in their pottery so that they could sell their merchandise at a higher price. More reputable merchants would hang a sign over their pottery — sine cera (without wax) — to inform customers that their merchandise was genuine. In other words, they were letting everyone know that they were not the type of merchant who would present a cheap fake or substitute as the real thing.

I would contend, with great pain I might add, that the practice and climate of most modern-day believers (and, therefore, churches) is a lot of talk about love but little to no genuine practice of love. Remember . . . sincere love is a characteristic of Kingdom Climate. So, if you see the weather of grudges being held against fellow believers, gossip gladly passed on under the guise of prayer requests, accusations about motives rather than giving each other the benefit of the doubt, attitudes we refuse to address, and lack of care or willingness to carry one another's burdens, then we have become "waxy" believers and it is easy to see or know that something is missing in the climate. That something is genuine and sincere love. We tend to substitute or, perhaps, even settle for telling each other once a week in a service that we love each other for sincere love. However, Paul is talking about a much deeper and more consistent, every day, moment-by-moment love that causes us to demonstrate it in every situation.

**Love must identify and verify.**

Jesus said that we would be known by our love. He states in John 13:35 that this is the thing that will identify and verify us as one of His. *"By this everyone will know that you are my disciples, if you love one another."* As believers, we like to talk about how love identifies us to the world. All too often, I think we fail to realize that it is our love that also helps believers identify believers, as well. Remember, Jesus tells us that everyone who says "Lord" isn't necessarily a true follower. In fact, in Matthew 7, Jesus is addressing false prophets. He lets us in on an important piece of information when He says that "by fruit, we know people." True for false prophets, but equally true for true believers. Love is the fruit that separates us and validates us! Our love is our brand - our mark. However, when we put out an inferior product, it reflects badly on the maker! **Waxy love makes us unidentifiable and undesirable.** If we don't have sincere love, then we are easily exposed as fake! Without sincere love, we are a **cheap substitute**.

In the 1990's, everyone pointed to a favorite TV sitcom as the epitome of what folks wanted. The theme song set the tone. When one of the regulars would enter the front door, the entire group of folks inside the club would actually act out the song. The song said, "Sometimes you want to go where everybody knows your name." When the slow-moving, folksy drunk walked in, everyone in the club would turn and yell his name, "Norm!" as a greeting. But even though the song was catchy, and it has been proven that the one-word people love hearing more than any other is their name, the truth is that just because everyone knows your name doesn't mean you have real or sincere love. Everyone can know your name and not really know you. Kingdom climate dictates that sincere love only takes place when we do daily life together. That is one of the reasons the church grew the way it did when it first began. Acts 2:46 (CSV) says, *"Every day they devoted themselves to meeting together in the temple, and broke bread from house to house."* The church grew because the men and women were practicing sincere love. They did life together daily. We have made it about attending a worship service once a week together. The end result is we feel lonely and disconnected. It is the daily exchange of care, concern, and love that produces a different weather pattern in our lives.

> KINGDOM CLIMATE DICTATES THAT SINCERE LOVE ONLY TAKES PLACE WHEN WE DO DAILY LIFE TOGETHER.

The saddest verse in the Bible is Psalms 142:4. David declares that he looked to the right and left, and there was no one to care for his soul. He experienced the void and absence of sincere love. God help us establish the climate of sincere love in our lives and in our churches.

**Love must bind.**

Love is the glue that is stronger than differences or distractions. We all have differences. Every relationship will be challenged by distractions. Sincere love binds us together enough that we can be real, vulnerable, and available. **It is love that makes Kingdom Climate safe!** Sincere love is exhibited when you defend a person when they aren't around. Love, without wax, takes place when you give someone grace even when they are obviously and, perhaps, even intentionally wrong and out of order. Paul, in Colossians 3:13 (NLT), says, *"Make allowance for each other's faults, and forgive anyone who offends you. Remember, the Lord forgave you, so you must forgive others."* Paul challenges us to make an allowance for each other's faults. Paul is exhorting us to practice sincere love in such a way that even if the person has done nothing to deserve it, we still make room for their mistakes! Surely, they should own their mistake first. Surely, they should admit their mistake first. No, Paul just says to approach our relationships with so much grace that we leave room for someone to choose the wrong word, use the wrong tone, do the wrong thing, or give the wrong look. Sincere love mandates an attitude of forgiveness before a wrong is committed or admitted.

In 1 Peter 4:8 (NIV), Peter chimes in when he says, *"Above all, love each other deeply, because love covers over a multitude of sins."*

This is a deep and sincere love. How deep? Love at a level that brings about the forgiveness of many sins. Love that covers sin and causes the offender to seek forgiveness rather than being crushed and cast out. Sincere love has nothing to do with liking one another. Think about the disciples for a moment. I am very confident that they may not have always liked one another. A fisherman and a zealot. A tax collector and taxpayer. A meek and mild and a loudmouth. What we see exemplified is that love is more important than like! Differences and distractions can be overcome! **Our like is about preference! Our love is being bound to one another!** In this day and age, we have allowed our like to become more important than our love. We need to flip the script. We must love one another! Love is something we choose to do. We love "in spite of." We love no matter what.

A.W. Tozer said, "The Bible teaches us that love is a benevolent principle and is under the control of our will. Love is the will to, the intention.

By that definition, it is possible to obey the divine command to love our neighbor. We may not in a thousand years be able to feel the surge of emotions toward certain neighbors, but we can go before God and solemnly will to love them, and love will come. Love is the love of willing, not the love of feeling!" There will be times when you won't feel like loving, but the question is not feeling; it is, are you willing to love at this level? Love that binds. Deeply. We fight against division rather than participating in it. Believing the best rather than the worst.

**Love must motivate.**

Love must motivate us to exert effort! The only way we can live up to the demands of this climate, to give the time necessary to participate in the climate, is if we love. If we don't love, then we won't work. If we don't love, then we won't try. If we don't love, then we won't sacrifice. If we don't love, then we won't extend ourselves.

Without love, we will settle for relationship with no fellowship or for fellowship with no relationship. We rub hearts but never rub elbows or vice versa. I remind you that when Jesus was 12 years old, He left His parents and went to the temple. Jesus' parents didn't even know He wasn't with them. They were in relationship, but at least in this moment, they weren't together or in fellowship. The fruit of sincere love is that we will be motivated to work for both . . . relationship and fellowship. Only love will cause you to give up time on an evening. Only love will cause you to forego something you want to do in order to do something with someone else. Love must motivate us to more than relationship, but also fellowship. Love must motivate us to more than just fellowship, but also relationship.

Tina Turner probably wouldn't have thought that the tune was catchy enough or the lyrics memorable enough to be a hit. She certainly couldn't have danced to this old hymn. But, perhaps, the truth of its lyrics is timely as it addresses Paul's challenge to love sincerely. I think, if nothing else, these stanzas speak to the depth of love that Paul called us to if we desire to establish a Kingdom Climate.

> Blest be the tie that binds
> Our hearts in Christian love;
> The fellowship our spirit finds

Is like to that above.

Before our Father's throne,

We pour our ardent prayers;

Our fears, our hopes, our aims are one—

Our comforts and our cares.

We share our mutual woes;

Our mutual burdens bear;

And often for each other flows

The sympathizing tear.

When we asunder part,

It gives us inward pain;

But we shall still be joined in heart,

And hope to meet again.

From sorrow, toil, and pain,

And sin we shall be free;

And perfect love and oneness reign

Through all eternity.

So, what's love got to do with it? Paul would quickly answer with one word and so should we . . . Everything!

# 10. PLAY YOUR CARDS RIGHT!

**Kingdom Climate Characteristic 4: Run from evil.**

Cell phone out in a flash. Video captured and posted. Viral in a moment. Tragedy, injury, and disaster streamed in hopes of gaining views. This phenomenon is a result of a shift that has taken place in our society. In days gone by, viewing these occasions was avoided. The impact, the damage, the break was blurred out so that the visual wouldn't be visible. Not anymore. Now all the bloody carnage, bones protruding, knee at weird angles, is not only broadcast, but they are on constant loops on social media. If the news refuses to show it, then we simply log on to other online resources to see what we missed. We no longer look away; we review. Our appetite for the stomach-turning highlights has grown. We know the wreck is coming, but we can't look away. Did you know this has been studied? Psychologists asked the question, "Why can't we look away?" One of the doctors, Dr. Renee Carr, concluded that "Humans are prone to negative bias and negative potency." "Negative bias is the tendency to automatically give more attention to a negative event and negative information than positive information or events." Simply stated, we tend to fixate on the negative.

When it comes to relationships, Paul must have known this would be our inclination. After demanding that we create a climate of sincere love, the very next characteristic of Kingdom Climate he gives us is found in the second half of Romans 12:9. Paul says, *"Run for dear life from evil; hold on for dear life to good."* I have no doubt that in this statement, Paul is definitely dealing with protecting our witness, testimony, and where we spend time and money. We can't get away from the fact that we must be careful about what we dwell on, watch, and listen to. However, we must remember that Paul is dealing with the climate of how we relate to one another. If we take this characteristic in context with what Paul has already said, then we can clearly see that **he is teaching us how to handle each other's mess!** If you don't believe that we have trouble with this, then why is it that when someone graduates college, gets a big promotion, or receives a huge blessing, there is no deluge of texts and Facebook posts? However, let a young lady get pregnant or let a young man get thrown behind bars for making a stupid decision, and the group texts begin. Our social media feeds explode. The whispers gather into shouts!

EMBRACING KINGDOM CLIMATE DOESN'T MEAN WE BURY OUR HEADS IN THE SAND AND IGNORE EVIL OR ACT LIKE IT DOESN'T EXIST IN EACH OTHER.

When we are dealing with each other, Paul confronts negative bias in us by saying that in order to shift to a Kingdom Climate, we should hang onto what is good. However, we must first understand that he prefaces this by saying run from evil. In other words, embracing Kingdom Climate doesn't mean we bury our heads in the sand and ignore evil or act like it doesn't exist in each other. However, we run from it. That sounds like a contradiction, doesn't it? We are supposed to run from evil and hang onto good. How do we do that?

Paul is teaching us that if **we are determined to have climate change, then we must make a conscious choice to focus our attention, hang onto, and believe what is good about the people around us.** It doesn't mean we don't see or ignore what is bad about them. However, it does mean that we can't fixate on that. It means we look to their good as we help them overcome the bad. It doesn't mean that we are afraid to address, confront, and challenge someone on the bad, to correct evil, or to call sin what it is. It doesn't mean we won't break fellowship if they refuse to repent and continue in self-destructive, open, and defiant sin. Why? Because we have genuine (sincere) love, and we can't let them continue to live in sin or be exposed to the danger of their current actions without saying something! Kingdom climate, which is founded on sincere love, dictates that in the process of calling out and holding one another accountable, we don't define someone by the bad but by the good. It is taking the approach that "I will believe the best about you!" Too many of us believe the worst first. We are too suspicious. Paul wants us to take an "I abhor and detest what is evil! But about you, I believe what is good, and I will cling to and call out the good in you!" position. He is calling us to adjust our focus point.

A wealthy couple desired to employ a chauffeur. The wife advertised, the applicants were screened, and four candidates were brought to her for the final selection. She called the prospective men to her balcony and pointed out a brick wall alongside the driveway. She asked the men, "How close do you think you could come to that wall without scratching my car?"

The first man felt he could drive within a foot of the wall without damaging the car. The second felt sure he could come within six inches. The third believed he could get within three inches. The fourth candidate said, "I do not know how close I could come to the wall without damaging your car. Instead, I would try to stay as far away from that wall as I could." The lady hired the fourth candidate. This candidate had a different focus. He understood that true skill in driving is not based on the ability to steer the car to a narrow miss as it is the ability to keep a wide margin of safety.

When we are developing Kingdom Climate in our lives, our focus must change. I no longer just spot the bad in those around me. If they are assigned to my life by God as a friend, mentor, mentee, pastor, or some other role, then I begin to pinpoint the good in them, and I hang on to that. The words Paul chose make this sound like a struggle. It sounds like a desperate attempt. Hang on for dear life. Stop and think about it just a moment . . . it is a fight; it is a struggle. We want to run to the wreck. We want to focus on the broken. But in order for our climate to change, we must hang on, fight to focus, and cling to what is good. When every instinct screams to let go and walk away. When every tendency shouts to believe the worst, when everyone else is posting the details about the disaster of someone's life, Paul says hang on. Refuse to let go. Grab the wheel and steer toward what is good.

We know if we hang around bad influence for too long, it will rub off on us and cause stormy weather to roll back in. It is clear that Paul gives instructions to cut and run at some point. But when? When we have hung on, clung to, defended, and believed the best about someone, how do we know when it is time to sever ties and run for our lives?

There are four characters with whom Jesus interacted that help us learn when to run and when to hang on - Judas, Peter, and the two thieves on the cross.

Judas and Peter were a lot alike in some ways. They were both Benedict Arnolds . . . backstabbers . . . betrayers. However, there is one major difference. Judas had a bad heart. Peter had a bad day! Judas was eaten up with betrayal. One day, under extreme pressure, Peter simply turned his back. Jesus teaches us that we run from Judas, but we restore Peter. Some of us struggle to see climate change because we get rid of the wrong people. We kick folks to the curb because they had a bad day. However, if they have a good heart, then we should extend grace and peace to them rather than deserting them. Some of us keep folks around that have good days, but their heart is corrupt. They didn't lie to us today. They didn't steal from us today. They didn't stab us in the back today. But what is their track record? We like their kisses today, but we can't ignore the knife in their hand tomorrow. We like their compliments. We like their attention. We like their flattery. But we can't treat Judas like Peter. If their heart is bad, then we must get rid of them. Learn their heart, or we will keep the wrong person and dismiss the right person or vice versa. To know their heart, we must dig deep. Jesus shows us that to learn someone's heart . . .

> **WE CAN'T TREAT JUDAS LIKE PETER. IF THEIR HEART IS BAD, THEN WE MUST GET RID OF THEM.**

We must listen to a person's words. Out of an abundance of the heart, the mouth speaks! When a person opens their mouth, they give us insight into who they are and whether we should run or hang on. The challenge is that most of us tend to ignore what we hear to our own demise. The truth is that if it continues to come out, then it isn't a bad day issue; it is a bad heart issue. Go back to the battlefield in the garden. Eve brings destruction because she didn't discern. Eve should have known she was talking to a snake because poison was coming out of its mouth. When we ignore the poison coming out of someone's mouth, we allow them to envenomate us. We can't continue treating snakes like sisters and boas like brothers. What's coming out of their mouth? There are only two options ... life or death. If it is gossip, rumors, anger, spite, criticism, etc., then they are a snake. Listen long and carefully, and you can hear the difference between sweet nothings and hissing!

Watch as Jesus uses this key to discern. Luke 23:39-43 (MSG):

> *One of the criminals hanging alongside cursed him: "Some Messiah you are! Save yourself! Save us!" But the other one made him shut up: "Have you no fear of God? You're getting the same as him. We deserve this, but not him—he did nothing to deserve this." Then he said, "Jesus, remember me when you enter your kingdom." He said, "Don't worry, I will. Today you will join me in paradise."*

The thieves had some similarities. They are both convicted criminals. They are guilty. This is probably not the first time they have been in trouble with the law. They have both been sentenced to death. They are both down to the last few moments of their life. They are both in pain. They are both having a bad day. They both start talking, and what comes out of their mouths allows Jesus to recognize that as similar as they were, they are very different. Although both were near, geographically speaking, they were, in fact, miles apart in their heart. By the words that came out of the repentant thief, Jesus was able to discern his heart!

When I was a kid, my mom absolutely loved Kenny Rogers' music. In fact, the only concert I ever remember Mom being interested in attending was his. Kenny Rogers' voice had the smoothness of a crooner mixed with just enough country twang to make him current. Now, to be honest, I have never really been a fan of country music. The mullet that I wore with pride until the early 2000s would probably give away that my preference in music was much more aligned with screaming electric guitars and driving drums. However, one of the songs that Kenny Rogers sang still sticks in my mind to this day. It wasn't until recently that I realized that the lyrics sound a lot like Paul's teaching about Kingdom Climate in Romans 12. Paul said run away from and hang on to. Kenny sang it like this . . . "You got to know when to hold them, know when to fold them. Know when to walk away and know when to run." The truth is the same. There are people who you need to hold tight. There are others that need to be discarded so that you can escape with your life! Don't be a gambler . . . learn the difference.

# 11. LIVE LIKE YOU ARE IN THE MOVIES!

**Kingdom Climate Characteristic 5: Live Loyal**

It is the scene that grabs us. Without realizing it, we hold our breath. Women weep freely while grown men fight back tears and claim previously nonexistent allergy conditions or swear that some mysterious dust has invaded the eye. These are the best moments of movies and books. It is the dog who refuses to leave the grave of its recently buried master. It is the soldier who will not leave the field of battle until he has risked his own life to drag his best friend out of harm's way. It is the friend who jumps in the car, skips the meeting that would set them up with untold fortunes simply because the friend in need must be reached regardless of money or miles. It is the warrior who is captured, tortured, and finally, at the point of death, with his last breath, still committed to the cause, he shouts "freedom" while his followers watch from the crowd helplessly. Moving in movies, but seemingly missing in life. Loyalty seems to be a lost, or at least rare, quality today. We no longer practice brand loyalty. Loyalty to a cause is fleeting and ends when pain enters the picture. Loyalty to family is questionable. Loyalty to employer . . . nonexistent. We have taken "To thine own self be true" as a way of living and operating in relationships. There just doesn't seem to be much loyalty to loyalty.

The word that Paul uses in his list of Kingdom Climate Characteristics isn't loyalty, but loyalty is what he is talking about! He says in Romans 12:10, *"Be devoted to one another in love."* Paul knew unless we can establish devoted loyalty with other believers, that the winds of division and distraction would swamp us. The word "devoted" that Paul chooses literally means to be concentrated on or to pursue. Pursuit through differences of opinion, differences of direction, and differences of preferences. Loyalty requires us to be committed to each other through thick or thin, good or bad, convenient or inconvenient, mountain top or valley. It means I am not around only as long as I can get something from you or if it is good for me. It means I am here for you for the long haul. It means conflict, feelings, or even arguments are not going to cause me to turn on you or walk away from you. I will give you the benefit of the doubt in all things. Why? Our relationship isn't just another relationship. You are part of me. We are members of the same body. I can't do without you any more than my physical body can't operate effectively without my nose or eye! You are essential for me. Therefore, I am loyal to you.

> LOYALTY REQUIRES US TO BE COMMITTED TO EACH OTHER THROUGH THICK OR THIN, GOOD OR BAD, CONVENIENT OR INCONVENIENT, MOUNTAIN TOP OR VALLEY.

There is an amazing account of loyalty in the Old Testament that illustrates this concept. Long before Paul ever penned these instructions, a young man by the name of Jonathan lived a life of loyalty. Jonathan's father was a madman by the name of Saul. However, as crazy as he was, he was also powerful. Saul was the king. This makes Jonathan a prince. He wasn't somewhere down the line in succession to the throne. He was next in line. If anything happens to Saul, then Jonathan will walk into the king's chamber as the man. He will take the throne. He will have unlimited power and authority, attention that would make a Hollywood celebrity envious, and riches that would make Bill Gates or Elon Musk duck their head in shame. All Jonathan has to do is sit silently on the sidelines and wait. His time will come. The only dilemma is that Jonathan was more loyal than he was ambitious.

Jonathan is best friends with a young man by the name of David. David is the rising superstar of the army. He has defeated a loudmouthed giant. He has escaped multiple attempts by Saul to kill him without retaliating because he was loyal, as well. In the end, Jonathan helps David dodge every attempt Saul makes on his life. He literally protects David, even though he knows that doing so will cost him the throne. This choice cost him. The price was high. He lost his father's approval. He endured his father's anger. He missed out on years of royal treatment. And he breaks the line of succession, not only for himself but for his own sons! If David becomes king, then the standard procedure of the day was all of Saul's descendants must be exterminated so that they don't threaten the throne.

Even with all of this knowledge, Jonathan, utilizing the gift of discernment, which helped him to know who to be loyal to rather than just blindly being loyal to his family, chose to be loyal to David. It was this loyalty that seals his legacy. To this day, we admire him for his selflessness. He is mentioned in the same sentences as David because he can't be separated from David's story, nor can he be separated from David's life. So, we can't forget about Jonathan. Neither could David. Even after Jonathan's untimely death, after David ascends to the throne, he still thinks about Jonathan's loyalty. This results in David seeking out Mephibosheth, Jonathan's son. He hunts him down. But don't get it twisted. Rather than following the example of the other kings of that era and executing this rightful successor to the throne, David follows Jonathan's example. Davide invites this "threat" to join him at the King's table for the rest of his life! Jonathan's son enjoys the new king's presence, provision, and protection due to the seed of loyalty his father had planted. Loyalty planted results in loyalty reaped. David's invitation to Mephibosheth shows us that the fruit of loyalty can transcend generations. The fruit of loyalty outlives us!

How loyal are we? Does the slightest offense break our relationship? Does a bad day or a word spoken in anger cause us to delete the contact forever from our phone? Does a cold shoulder turn into a frozen future for our relationship? Paul is trying to teach us that loyalty produces Kingdom Climate in our lives. He knew it was the relationships that have endured storms and testing that would be the relationships that pull us through weather that is sinking everyone else around us. We can have at least one person who is "Jesus with skin on" that we can lean on, cling to, and fight for rather than against.

I sat at a table with a trusted advisor. I was waiting for him to drop the bomb on me. I had asked him to tell me the truth. "What is my biggest flaw? What is my biggest weakness as a pastor? What is it that you see in me that gets me in the most trouble?" My friend is as blunt as he is honest. He looked at me and said, "Steve, your biggest issue is that you are loyal to a fault. You hold on to people even if they are hurting you and causing your demise." I couldn't respond. I simply nodded my head. As I began to process what he had just said and reviewed the relationships in my life, I came to a conclusion. I decided that if loyalty was what brings about pain or even my own failure, demise, or even destruction, then I would choose loyalty. A couple of years removed from that discussion, I can assure you that there have been times when loyalty has hurt. I probably endured some pain because I failed to operate with the discernment necessary to know who to be loyal to. There have been moments when I have had to choose the success of someone else over my own success. I have had to decide that someone else being healthy was more important to me than me being scarred as a result. I believe that this loyalty will ultimately pay dividends and, like on the day David remembered Jonathan, will result in favor, if not for me, then for my children and my grandchildren. I know not everyone approves of loyalty. However, I am convinced that Paul does, and, more importantly, I know Jesus does! The One who was faithful till the end applauds loyalty. In fact, in Revelation 21:13, we are told that *"he that endures till the end shall be saved!"* Remaining loyal carries a high price tag, and it carries an equally high payoff!

We began this chapter by talking about movies. There is a noteworthy line in what is considered by many a cinematic masterpiece. I am probably not in that camp. However, I do believe one of the main characters got it right. Don Vito Corleone, in *The Godfather*, said, "The strength of a family, like the strength of an army, lies in its loyalty to each other."

# 12. ON YOUR FEET!

**Kingdom Climate Characteristic 6: Show Honor**

Just one of the neighborhood kids. He grew up playing games with the other kids on the narrow streets of the village. He most likely slept over at his best friend's home. Everyone knew him. He knew everyone. It is the way of a small town. However, the young man grew up and left the comfortable confines of his town. He walks out and becomes well known . . . famous, in fact! He is "big time." He is a showstopper. He can do feats that shock the mind. His abilities cause people to blink. The people exclaim that if they hadn't seen it with their own eyes, then they wouldn't have believed it. The young man has a following. People are constantly inviting him to their homes, banquets, and feasts. When he is on the guest list, the ticket to the party becomes hard to find. Now, after all of his success, acclaim, and achievements, a hometown hero is about to come home. You would expect parades, keys to the city will surely be awarded, and speeches will be made; without a doubt, the young miracle worker will be asked to share some of his abilities with folks he used to live by, shop with, and attend school. What hero wouldn't want to do that in his hometown?

If you stop and read closely, you discover one of the most profound statements recorded in the New Testament is about such a homecoming! Jesus is the hometown hero. He is back in the community in which He grew up. Now, the Son of God, who has the power to raise the dead, heal the sick with one touch or one word, and the ability to turn tap water into the finest drink ever served at a wedding, is walking down Main Street.

In Mark 6:5 (NIV), the Bible says, *"Jesus could not do any miracles there, except lay His hands on a few sick people and heal them."* On the streets where He played marbles, whistled at the neighbor girl, and played with the neighbor kids, this powerful miracle worker is powerless. How is this even possible? Was the people's unbelief stronger than Jesus? No way! He isn't just a hometown boy; He is God in the flesh. He has all power! Perhaps we should notice what isn't said in the Bible. It doesn't say Jesus didn't want to do miracles. There is no lack of desire mentioned. No lack of compassion. No lack of anything except power? You can't find anywhere else in Scripture where Jesus' power was limited or diminished. He has walked boldly, with power to spare, into villages just like this one. Now, in His hometown, does something go wrong? Did Jesus just have a bad day? What's going on here? Jesus finally makes a revealing statement that explains what is going on in this odd and unexpected scene. Jesus said, *"A prophet has little honor in his hometown, among his relatives, on the streets he played in as a child."* Could it be true that because the folks in town knew Him so well that they were filled with contempt? Were their minds full of statements they didn't dare say with their mouth? "That is just Joseph and Mary's boy. Who does He think He is? I remember Him when He had pimples!" God literally walks into a town and can't help the people He knew best because His help was undermined by their lack of honor!

> YOU CAN'T FIND ANYWHERE ELSE IN SCRIPTURE WHERE JESUS' POWER WAS LIMITED OR DIMINISHED.

This astonishing account is also heartbreaking. It is heartbreaking because a lack of honor cost Jesus' hometown so much. They missed their opportunity to hear the good news. They missed their chance to see the Kingdom of Heaven invade their community. This account should serve as a reminder that honor is a key to seeing Kingdom Climate come into our lives. Paul jumps on the idea of honor very quickly in Romans 12. In verse three, Paul lays the foundation for this climate-altering trait when he says:

> *And because of God's gracious gift to me I say to every one of you: Do not think of yourself more highly than you should. Instead, be modest*

*in your thinking, and judge yourself according to the amount of faith that God has given you. (GNT)*

Why would he tell us to be careful about thinking too much of ourselves? Paul knew that if we think too highly of ourselves, then we will never be able to honor someone above ourselves. We would never be willing to play second fiddle. We would never be able to come to the place where we would not only applaud but also assist someone else to succeed, even if doing so means that I am not noticed or promoted. We would be tempted to snub the hometown hero because we grew up with them. So, Paul begins the lesson, and, for emphasis, he drives it home again in straight-to-the-point language.

Romans 12:10 (NIV)

*"Be devoted to one another in love. Honor one another above yourselves."*

Honor is a recurring theme in Scripture. Just in the New Testament alone, every age bracket, socioeconomic status, and level of relationship is addressed when it relates to honor. Children are commanded to honor their parents. Wives are instructed to honor their husbands. Employees are told to honor their boss. The body of Christ is told to honor those who labor among you. You simply cannot escape the demand for honor as Kingdom Climate. Paul was adamant! We must establish a culture of honor because he knew this... God's blessings are found in a climate of honor. **Honor is not about position . . . it is about life source.** If you go back and look at the list of who is supposed to be honored, then you discover that **we are instructed to honor anyone who is a life source (parents, spouse, boss, volunteers).**

This is a significant deviation from our society's climate of a "dog eat dog," fight for what is my right, finish first, self-promotion, and cancel culture. The climate of honor operates from the premise that everyone is essential. Everyone is important. Everyone matters. We must treat each other as a life source. Everyone around me has the potential to bring life to me. Often, the destructive climate of our lives can be traced back to a lack of honor. We simply didn't value or prefer someone over ourselves. We allowed disrespect to come into our hearts or our heads. The result is we treat others in such a way that they feel devalued. Either their exit or their explosive response produces chaos and pain in our lives.

There is an account in the Old Testament that, perhaps, best illustrates the importance of honor for us. In 1 Samuel 16, the prophet Samuel was tasked with anointing the next king who would reign in place of God-forsaken Saul. Samuel follows God's instructions to go to the house of a man named Jesse. When Samuel arrives and states his business, Jesse quickly assembles his large brood of sons. He marches them in front of Samuel, expecting the prophet to choose one of his oldest and strongest. He places the All-Stars in front of Samuel. However, the parade of Jesse's prodigies drags on until not only has Samuel passed on the first, but also the seventh. Samuel never once uncorks the flask of oil to announce the new king. Samuel gets to the end of the lineup and, in desperation, asks Jesse, "Are these all of your sons?" Wait a minute. Think about this for a moment. Surely, a father wouldn't think so little of any of his sons that he would leave one out. But, sure enough, the youngest was absent. The runt was out in the back pasture or in the wilderness somewhere, watching the sheep.

Go back and read the account. You discover that God still hasn't let Samuel in on the secret that this overlooked son was the chosen one. However, notice that when Samuel is told there is one final son, they would have to go find him and bring him back to the house. Samuel refuses to sit down until this sheep keeper named David has arrived. Matthew Henry writing about this moment gives insight into Samuel's potential mindset, "We will not sit down to meat till he come hither; for, if all the rest be rejected, this must be he. He that designed not to sit at table at all is now waited for as the **principal** guest." Samuel has passed over all the other possibilities and refuses to show a lack of honor just in case this young man is the one. How many of us sit down on what God has anointed? The result of lack of honor is that the appointed and anointed never arrives! The appointed king can't walk in if we are sitting down. **Our refusal to honor results in the absence of anointed folks in our life.** We must learn that it is honor that makes room for and pulls the anointing into our life.

Often, God will send us WHAT WE NEED in a package WE DO NOT WANT or even LIKE. David wasn't packaged like Samuel expected. If Samuel had not been operating in the Kingdom Climate characteristic of honor, then he would have allowed dishonor to disqualify him from receiving the gift that was in David. How many of us miss or even reject

God because we forget that God uses surrogates? His representative may not be what or who we anticipated! Honor forces us to dig beyond our own expectations and preferences to see God in people regardless of their race, gender, skill, education, or talent.

Honor will require us to fight our own preferences. This means that although I prefer to do things solo and may be capable of doing them better than you, I will honor you and give you a shot. This means that although I prefer the best parking spot closest to the door, I honor you and leave space for you. Honor causes me to do my best to help your dream come true. I quit fighting for my own blessing and do everything in my ability to make sure you are blessed. This battle with preference must be ongoing. Paul's admonishment to "outdo one another in preferring one another" strikes a death blow to our preferences, becoming our strongest prison!

> **HONOR WILL REQUIRE US TO FIGHT OUR OWN PREFERENCES.**

We want to rail against the weather of loneliness, apathy, anger, and hurt feelings, but are we willing to work to establish a Kingdom Climate of honor so that our life will go well? It is easier to bail when we aren't served. It is easier to get mad and sulk when someone takes our spot or someone else is blessed. It is more enjoyable to throw a tantrum when I don't get to sing when I want and with whom I want. It is tempting to hear something bad about someone and use it as ammo to make me feel better about myself, at their expense. However, it is honor, at the expense and sacrifice of our preferences, which will produce a weather change in our lives. We must learn that we are really showing honor to our King when we honor the King's servants who are around us. Our honor isn't really given to flesh and blood but to God. This is what David learned and modeled. Somewhere, David learned that honor matters to God. It was why he refused to touch Saul even when Saul was out of his mind with jealousy. Time and time again, David had opportunities to take matters into his own hands, kill Saul, and be elevated to the position of King that he had already been anointed to take. Yet, out of honor, He refused! He knew that honor for the king was right because he was honoring THE KING by having respect for Saul.

Are you sitting down? Refuse to sit down until someone with a kingly anointing is in the room. Get on your feet!

# 13. I AM DISNEYLAND!

**Kingdom Climate Characteristic 7: Be Joyful**

Stop what you are doing. Hurry! Pick up your phone and dial 911. I need you to report a theft! You may not even realize it, but we have been robbed. This heist took place decades ago, in 1955 when Walt Disney opened Disneyland and attached the slogan to this adventure park . . . "The happiest place on earth!" The use of that slogan in reference to a theme park with roller coasters and bumper cars should offend and anger us. If it doesn't do that, then it should certainly highly motivate us. This slogan should have been captured, tweaked, and utilized by not only the Church but by each of us as believers in Christ. Paul clearly states Kingdom Climate is a climate filled with joy! In other words, we are Disneyland! The tweak would simply be "We are the most joy-full place on earth!"

Paul makes it clear in Romans 12:12 when he emphatically states, *"Be joyful in hope!"* He is telling us that the climate of our life changes when the climate of our life is joy-full! Our life should literally be a joy ride! The wise man in Ecclesiastes forewarned us in his examination of life that it was going to be a wild ride of tears and laughter, birth and death, killing and healing . . . a total of 29 mutually opposed seasons that jerk us and clank us through the ride of life. High highs and low lows. And most of the time, most of us just wish things would level out! We wish for this because our joy level is so often tied to the direction of our lives. When we are up, our joy level is high. When we are down, there is no joy to be found. Even though in children's church we sang we had the "joy, joy, joy down in our heart to stay," we live an almost Dr. Jekyll/Mr. Hyde experience. It is into this wild ride that Jesus walks onto the scene and, in one statement, reveals that He can level things out. We love this statement but often fail to really dig into the means to obtain what Jesus is offering. Listen to what He says in John 15:11 . . .

*"I have told you this so that my joy may be in you and that your joy may be complete."* (NIV)

*"I've told you these things for a purpose: that my joy might be your joy, and your joy wholly mature."* (MSG)

*"These things have I spoken unto you, that my joy might remain in you, and that your joy might be full."* (KJV)

Those of us who struggle with living joy-full often fixate on Jesus' statement that He can make our joy complete and mature. We sit around and wait for Him to accomplish this in our lives as we continue to experience the harrowing corners and cliff-like drop-offs. The gut-churning twists and turns in our lives make us question if maybe Jesus has shortchanged us or is unable to fulfill His promises. We grab onto the promise of complete joy and never stop to read the first part of His statement. Jesus says He told us some things "on purpose" that determine whether or not our joy can be complete. So, let's back up and hear what He says will determine our joy level.

In John 15:1-10 (MSG), Jesus says . . .

> *I am the Real Vine and my Father is the Farmer. He cuts off every branch of me that doesn't bear grapes. And every branch that is grape-bearing he **prunes** back so it will bear even more. You are already pruned back by the message I have spoken. "**Live in me.** Make your home in me just as I do in you. In the same way that a branch can't bear grapes by itself but only by being joined to the vine, you can't bear fruit unless you are joined with me. "I am the Vine, you are the branches. When you're joined with me and I with you, the relation intimate and organic, the harvest is sure to be abundant. Separated, you can't produce a thing. Anyone who separates from me is deadwood, gathered up and thrown on the bonfire. But if you make yourselves at home with me and my **words are at home in you**, you can be sure that whatever you ask will be listened to and*

*acted upon. This is how my Father shows who he is—when you produce grapes, when you mature as my disciples. "I've loved you the way my Father has loved me. Make yourselves at home in my love. If you **keep my commands**, you'll remain intimately at home in my love. That's what I've done—kept my Father's commands and made myself at home in his love. (Emphases are mine.)*

Our joy level is based on whether or not we will embrace the prerequisites of having joy! I emphasized these prerequisites by making them bold in the text. Jesus says our joy is determined by our willingness to be pruned! In other words, Jesus makes it clear that our Father, in our best interest, will make cuts in our lives. In other words, He will remove things. Most of us are thankful for the additions that God makes in our life. However, I have discovered in my own life and in the lives of so many other joyless people that most of us are unwilling to accept cuts or subtractions. We have joy until God removes something. As long as He is adding things, we are smiling and dancing through life. However, it is when He removes something or someone, especially if we like that thing or someone He has determined is stunting our growth, that most of us become angry, despondent, depressed, and even tempted to walk out of the vineyard altogether.

> OUR JOY LEVEL IS BASED ON WHETHER OR NOT WE WILL EMBRACE THE PREREQUISITES OF HAVING JOY!

Let a death come that we didn't want to come, and we lose our joy. Let a breakup take place when we thought this was "the one." Let a firing take place when we thought we were going to get a promotion. Let a zig come when we anticipated a zag, and we not only don't have joy, we become grumpy and disgruntled. Simply stated, we like an adding God but often resist a cutting God. Jesus reveals to us that our joy will be dependent on trusting God enough to know that Father knows best. He alone is uniquely qualified to know what or who needs to be removed from our lives! Some of us have no joy because we fight these cuts. We hang on to things/people that God was trying to remove so that our joy could be full!

Jesus also points out (and this one is really hard to accept) that God doesn't just cut when things are going bad. He actually says there are times when we are bearing fruit that He will step in and prune. Right at the time when we thought everything was going as good as it could go. Right when we were making a name for ourselves, getting noticed, and enjoying life, Jesus says that God will unsheathe His knife and perform surgery on us so that we can bear even more fruit. So often, we forget that God isn't really concerned about our comfort as much as He is concerned about our character.

Jesus says our "joy-fullness" is determined by whether or not we are rooted. We quote Acts 17:28, "*In Him we live, move and have our being*," but is that how we live?" Jesus, on purpose, so that we can have full joy, uses the language of connection. He says, live in me, rooted, connected; make your home in me, intimate. In using those words, He drives home the fact that our life separated from Him cannot be full of joy! We want Jesus to be the basis of our church life. However, we must also allow Him to have access to our home, work, and leisure life!

How do we know if we are rooted and connected and if our life is positioned in Him? How do we know that we are set up for full joy? It is easier to claim rootedness than it is to actually live up to the two standards that Jesus gives us, which reveal if we are actually rooted. I think the order in which He mentions these two standards is interesting. He says we are positioned for the fullness of joy when His Words are at home in us. Our level of joy is directly proportional to the Word that has made its home in us. No Word = No Joy. Little Word = Little Joy. Much Word = Much Joy. The Holy Spirit makes the Word more than ink on a page. The Holy Spirit makes the Word come alive in us. We read, and the Holy Spirit roots the truth in us, and the fruit it produces is joy!

David understood the connection of joy with God's Word. In Psalm 119:28, he wrote, "*I weep with sorrow; encourage me by your word.*" David knew that God's Word is what brings encouragement and joy, even when he was weeping in sorrow. David taught his son this truth. David said to Solomon:

> *My son, attend to my words; incline your ear unto my sayings. Let them not depart from your eyes; keep them in the midst of your heart. For they are life unto those that find them, and health to all their flesh."* (Proverbs 4:20-22)

David wanted Solomon to know that God's Word, kept in His heart, is what produces life and health. A Wordless life can't help but be a joyless life. It is when, and only when, our lives become a residence for His Word that we can find real and lasting joy. Only His Word can bring joy in the mourning. Only His Word can wipe sorrow away! Only His Word brings life!

Second, Jesus gives us one more standard to check that determines if we are able to experience the fullness of joy. He says we will become full of joy when we **become obedient to His commands.** In other words, our joy is dependent on and determined by our obedience. You would think those of us who are parents would understand this concept. However, for some reason, we seem surprised when our life is full of disobedience and void of joy. Think about your own experience at home. As a parent or as a child, is your life full of joy when there is disobedience in the equation? NO! Whether you are the one being disobeyed or the one disobeying, the result is the same - turmoil and usually punishment/pain. Likewise . . . when we fail to obey, there is no platform for sustained joy. When we are full of disobedience, we can't expect to be full of joy! It is almost comical at times to talk to people who are struggling and are down in the dumps. I say that because the root of their lack of joy can almost always be traced to an area of disobedience. Yet, we never seem to make the connection! Obedience is a key component for joy!

In His declaration that He can give us fullness of joy, Jesus issues a wake-up call or challenge. If He can make our joy full, whole, and complete, it stands to reason that this must also mean that our joy can be less than full. It is logical to conclude that if fullness of joy is available, it is possible to live at a joy level below what is available. We know this happens because we see the results around us. The result is soured Christians. I have heard these types of Christians described as people who look like a mule who sucked a golf ball out of a gofer hole. Now, to be honest, I have never seen a mule suck a golf ball out of a gofer hole. However, I can imagine the sour look of that face because I have seen it modeled on the faces of believers who haven't experienced Jesus' joy level. The fact is, as followers of Christ who have access to the fullness of joy, our countenance should testify of His goodness even before we testify with our words. This is what St. Francis of Assisi was talking about when he said, "Preach the Gospel at all times, and if necessary, use words." You may say, "Well, I am melancholy. I am kind of a downer. That is just my personality." So, what you are saying then is that your personality is your idol! His power should overtake and override our personality. If our joy is a gift from God, then it should be evident in our bodies and on our faces!

Joy is an essential component of Kingdom Climate because it sets us apart and produces strength in us. David declares in Psalm 45:7 (NIV), *"You love righteousness and hate wickedness; therefore God, your God, has set you above your companions by anointing you with the oil of joy."* Think about that for a moment. We often talk about people being anointed to preach, anointed to sing, anointed to pray, but David declares that **we are anointed with joy!** This anointing for joy doesn't depend on personality or even circumstances. Joy is dependent on God's anointing on our life. This anointing of joy should be evident in our lives. David declares this joy is what should set us apart from our companions. Nehemiah and, the writer of I Chronicles, assures us that joy makes us strong. Nehemiah 8:10 (NIV) says that the *"Joy of the Lord is our strength."* I Chronicles 16:27 (NIV) says, *"Splendor and majesty are before him; strength and joy ARE in his dwelling place."*

Notice that wherever joy exists, strength follows. If you don't think joy can make you strong, I want to remind you of what the Hebrew writer tells us in Hebrews 12:1-2 (NIV):

> *And let us run with perseverance the race marked out for us, fixing our eyes on Jesus, the pioneer and perfecter of faith. For the joy set before him he endured the cross, scorning its shame, and sat down at the right hand of the throne of God.*

Jesus was strong enough to endure the cross and all the shame associated with it because of joy. Jesus' joy was found in obedience to the mission that His Father had given Him. He could endure excruciating torture because He knew He was fulfilling the will of His Father. **If Jesus' joy enabled Him to face death, then surely His joy in you can empower you to face life!**

David once again helps us when he states in Psalm 16:11 (KJV), *"You will show me the path of life; In Your presence is fullness of joy; At Your right hand are pleasures forevermore."* David has a revelation that when we are trying to establish the Kingdom Climate of joy, location is everything.

David is adamant that the only place to find fullness of joy is found in the presence of The King. David had learned that happiness is the product of condition. Joy is the product of location. The difference is that simple.

Happiness is defined by the condition of your life. If your condition changes, then your happiness changes. Happiness is made up of two words that literally mean "happenstance"! Happiness comes from the root word "hap," which means an event or a happening. What this presupposes is that happiness is based on the occurrence of an event. We know that the impact of an event will change based on varying circumstances. This means that happiness is based on the occasion of an event that has no guarantee of producing a positive emotion. So, happiness fluctuates; it comes and goes. The reason so many of us are up and down, in and out, on the top of the mountain one day and submerged in the swamp of discouragement the next day is that we have based our outlook on condition rather than location. We have settled for a cheap, government-promised right to pursue happiness. Even when we find it, it only lasts for a short amount of time. It lasts until the car's new smell wears off. It is sustained until the relationship comes to a heartbreaking end. It lingers until we taste defeat rather than victory. Happiness is secure until the dream job turns into a nightmare or until the best friend becomes our worst enemy. Happiness is fleeting and temporary because happiness is a condition. Therefore, the condition has to continually be conditioned.

But that isn't joy. Joy has nothing to do with condition. It is a location. When we get the location correct, the conditions don't matter. Joy is found in the location of God's presence. In His presence, joy is sustained and secure because God never changes. He never fluctuates. Never decreases. Never wavers. So, our joy-fullness can remain consistent regardless of what is going on around us. The source of our joy isn't located in friends, possessions, and popularity. Our joy is firmly found in His presence.

> JOY HAS NOTHING TO DO WITH CONDITION. IT IS A LOCATION.

I used to tell young people that they should sell tickets because their spiritual lives were so up and down that they looked like a roller coaster. This statement was an indictment against the wishy- washiness of so many young believers. I believe that we can be much more stable and consistent than this. However, I am also convinced we should be able to sell "joy rides" to those around us. This ride won't look like the loopy, corkscrew, sharp drop-off rides that caused Walt Disney to lay claim to the happiest place on earth. Instead, whether we are experiencing the highest moments or the lowest moments, regardless of whether we are at the top of the mountain or in the depths of a valley, our ride is steady. Our ride is strong. So, from a joy-full life, let it ring out loud and proud . . . "Tickets! Get your tickets here! All aboard." People will stand in line for this ride!

# 14. PAIN PARTNERS

**Kingdom Climate Characteristic 8: Practice Patience**

Jumbo shrimp. Virtual reality. Student teacher, Working vacation. Civil war. If you were paying attention in your high school English Class, then you probably know these are examples of what is called an "Oxymoron." An oxymoron is a combination of words with contradictory meanings. Even though the words are often antonyms (words with opposite meanings), they don't negate each other. In fact, I will use one of these in the next chapter... deafening silence. In his list of Kingdom Climate characteristics, Paul uses what appears to be an oxymoron when he combines the words patient and affliction in Romans 12:12 (NIV) when he says, "Be joyful in hope, **patient in affliction**, faithful in prayer." Even the word affliction sounds painful. I don't know about you, but whenever I have experienced anything even close to affliction, I would not use the word "patient" to describe my attitude or disposition. When I stump my toe, have a hangnail, or get a splinter, patience isn't a word I would associate with my demeanor at that moment. The words just seem to contradict each other.

Paul is teaching us that they don't negate one another. He is instructing us that it is not only necessary but also possible to monitor and control our attitude when we are in the middle of painful moments. He is showing us that we can continue to operate in grace even when in pain by focusing on the trustworthiness of our God. He teaches us how to endure hardships and pain. Patiently waiting, we are strengthened by the knowledge that God can't be anything less than faithful to us! That seems like a pretty straightforward truth, even if it isn't an easy one to practice. However, I think that Paul's teaching goes beyond just how we respond to our own pain. Remember, he has just pushed us to be full of joy, not a happiness that is determined by our health, our freedom, or any other circumstance. Constant and consistent joy. So, if that Kingdom Climate Characteristic has become a reality in our life, then an affliction or no affliction really doesn't dictate our attitude. So, Paul, if the affliction really doesn't have the ability to impact our joy-filled life and outlook, why are you telling us that we have to be patient in affliction?

Let me see if a question might shed light on why I think Paul includes this in his list. Have you ever been impatient with someone who is struggling? It could be a financial need, an emotional need, or even a physical challenge. Regardless of the type of need, or in Paul's language . . . affliction, it seems like all the person can focus on is THEIR pain! All they seem to talk about, post on social media, pray about, and dominate the conversation with is their affliction. Come on, admit it . . . you have avoided them, right? You have hidden their posts, haven't you? Don't deny it; you saw their number pop up on your phone screen and intentionally allowed the call to go to voicemail. This person is so consumed and obsessed by their own need that they are oblivious to the needs of anyone else around them. Several years ago, at the young age of 46, I had an unexpected heart attack. From that eventful day for well over a year, whether I meant for it to happen or not, I would find myself in every conversation and in every situation, bringing up my "heart attack story." It was like I couldn't forget about it and needed to talk about it. I believe that experience helped me to better understand what Paul was saying. Paul is telling us that Kingdom Climate is one in which I am patient when you are going through affliction. Do we need to be patient when we are in pain? Certainly! The strength of our joy helps us address pain! It is when we run into someone else who is overtaken by affliction that we most need to operate in the climate of patience.

> KINGDOM CLIMATE IS ONE IN WHICH I AM PATIENT WHEN YOU ARE GOING THROUGH AFFLICTION.

If we would remember that **not everyone is as blessed as we are right now,** it would help us to offer grace to Debbie Downer and Negative

Neal when it seems they live with constant complaints. Not everyone is as victorious or recovered as we are right now. There are some around us who are in a struggle, and they are fighting for their life. If you don't establish a Kingdom Climate, then you will grow impatient with those who aren't overcoming and winning as fast as you would like. There are some struggles and hard times that are going to take an extended amount of time for people to exit. Be patient. Yes, some people stagnate in trials and should have already moved on and need to be encouraged to do so. Some people are like the children of Israel who circled too long. We all know people, even believers, who seem to have the ability to turn an 11-day trip into 40 years of circling. They turn pit stops into parking lots. This fact can be annoying and off-putting, to say the least. We (OK, really, it is just me) want to shout from the rooftop, "Just move on! Get over it already!" But we must remember that Kingdom Climate is filled with the hope and belief that one day, they, too, will walk into their promise, destiny, calling, and purpose. It is our patience not only with our own affliction but with theirs that will ultimately encourage them to keep walking and moving towards wholeness. We wait expectantly with them.

I am reminded of Jesus' response to someone in affliction. We know this person as the "woman with the issue of blood." Her affliction had labeled and marked her. Her affliction had cost her everything, even her dignity. Everywhere she went, she had to identify herself by crying out "unclean." It cost her relationships. Intimacy with a husband, children, or neighbors. An outcast. It cost her future. She had spent all she had. No intimacy with her heavenly Father. Her affliction disqualified her from entrance into the temple. God must have seemed unreachable during this drawn-out and dire 12-year affliction. I am sure this affliction was always on the tip of her tongue. I am sure it consumed her thoughts and conversations held at a distance. So, in a moment of desperation, she breaks the law. She quietly presses through the crowd that had probably become impatient with her issue. She sneaks up on Jesus and touches His garment. In that moment, her affliction has, by religious law, affected and immediately inconvenienced Jesus.

Because she is unclean, now Jesus is unclean and will be required to go into isolation and ritual bathing before He can once again move around in public or go to the temple to worship. I am sure that when Jesus stopped and asked who touched Him, this little lady was terrified. She knew what she had done was not allowed. She had most likely accidentally touched others in her past and felt the sting of rebuke and the curses of those who now had to adjust their calendar because of her carelessness. I am sure she was expecting a stern and embarrassing remark at best, or perhaps even a physical rebuke from Jesus. In fact, Scripture tells us when she falls at Jesus' feet, she is trembling in fear. Why fear? I am convinced that the response of impatient people over the years has caused her to expect more impatience. She finally owns up to what she has done. Instead of anger, Jesus simply responds, "Go in peace". I know she went away in peace because she was healed of her affliction. However, I wonder if a portion of her peace was a result of someone who interacted with her with patience and grace.

> WE NEED TO INSERT PATIENCE INTO OUR INTERACTIONS WITH THOSE WHO ARE SUFFERING.

Perhaps these conflicting words are a wake-up call to some of us. We need to insert patience into our interactions with those who are suffering. We need to be more understanding. We must have hope, not just for our answer and solution, but for theirs, as well. We need to exercise faith, not just for our healing and provision, but for those who are currently in pain. We can do this because we recognize that if God did it for us, then He will do it for someone else, too. We become partners in pain. We don't cause the pain or exploit the pain. Neither do we ignore the pain. We simply join them on their journey to wholeness and freedom. We become pain partners by walking through the fire with them. Holding their hand. Hearing their hurt. We may not have an immediate solution, but we do have a shoulder. The word "patient" Paul uses in this verse is the Greek word "hypomeno". It is a verb that means "to remain; not recede or flee; to persevere; under misfortunes and trials to hold fast to one's faith in Christ; to endure, bear bravely and calmly ill-treatments." I often wonder if the reason folks in pain don't believe that Jesus can help them is because they have confused our response with Jesus'? I think this is why Paul is adamant that we develop a climate of patience in affliction. This climate helps us remain when everyone else deserts. We don't recede, flee from, unfriend, avoid, or block the calls of those who are hurting and in pain. Our presence in the pain assures our hurting brothers and sisters of His presence. By the way, Paul inserts this characteristic right before two other characteristics that further illustrate how we practice this commanded patience. He tells us to partner with those in pain by being faithful in prayer and by sharing with those in need.

If we are going to operate in Kingdom Climate, we must listen when we are tired of hearing the repeated story and diagnosis. We must answer the call, even though we know it will cost us the next 30 minutes of our lives. What we may discover is that as we remain patient in affliction, folks who touch us may actually touch Jesus! And that, my friend, would be… awfully good! (See what I did there?)

# 15. WALL WARS

**Kingdom Climate Characteristic 9: Pray Faithfully**

In 1990, a great theologian burst on the scene. This "preacher" was different. His moves were different. His dress was different. His sermon was delivered over a cadence called rap and featured synchronized dancers and shiny jewelry. MC Hammer stepped up to the mic and dropped this truth on the world . . . "We've got to pray just to make it today!" OK, maybe Hammer wasn't a profound theologian, but he was a great performer. His signature, super baggy pants and crazy dance moves made his message palatable, even if not practiced by millions. Although his conclusion was correct, I am not really sure that the song, even with its catchy rhythm and beat, ever resulted in a dramatic move toward prayer. Paul would have agreed with Hammer. In Romans 12:12 (NIV), Paul simply said, with no drums or dancers in the background, *"(Be) faithful in prayer."* Different delivery than Hammer's, but the same message. Prayer is an important component of Kingdom Climate, and yet, so many of us struggle in this area. As one man said, "Of all the duties enjoined by Christianity, none is more essential and yet more neglected than prayer."

Paul certainly would not be in favor of believers omitting prayer from the climate of their lives. However, it is interesting that prayer is this far down his list. Shouldn't prayer be the first component of Kingdom Climate? Why did Paul push it so far down? Why does Paul wait until the end of Romans 12:12 after he has listed eight other Kingdom Climate Characteristics to say, "(Be) faithful in prayer."? Could it be that Paul wanted us to realize that too often, we put the establishment of Kingdom Climate off on God rather than stepping into an active role as participants with God? "Waiting on God" sounds spiritual, but it is often nothing more than a convenient excuse to never start the hard work of changing the climate. I don't think Paul's purpose in placing prayer deeper down the list is his attempt to diminish the necessity of prayer. I simply think Paul is saying the things he has mentioned before; his admonition to be faithful in prayer will require prayer-bathed and prayer-fueled action.

The importance of prayer can certainly be found in the life of Jesus. Perhaps it is never more noticeable than in Luke 5.

Luke 5:12-16 (NIV)

> *One day in a certain village he was visiting, there was a man with an advanced case of leprosy. When he saw Jesus, he fell to the ground before him, face downward in the dust, begging to be healed. "Sir," he said, "if you only will, you can clear me of every trace of my disease." Jesus reached out and touched the man and said, "Of course I will. Be healed." And the leprosy left him instantly! Then Jesus instructed him to go at once without telling anyone what had happened and be examined by the Jewish priest. "Offer the sacrifice Moses' law requires for lepers who are healed," he said. "This will prove to everyone that you are well." Now the report of his power spread even faster and vast crowds came to hear him preach and to be healed of their diseases. But he often withdrew to the wilderness for prayer.*

This is an incredible account, but because of the mind-boggling act of grace and the miracle that was produced, we can easily miss the prayer component of Jesus's life. This may be because Luke mentions it in a manner that makes prayer almost come off as an afterthought. But slow down and read the last verse again, *"But He often withdrew to the wilderness for prayer."* Did you see the key word? Often. One version says, "as was His custom." Jesus had established the Kingdom Climate of faithful prayer in His life. He OFTEN withdrew to pray. What you do often is what fills you! How often do you set time aside, schedule aside, career aside, entertainment aside, hobbies aside, and pray?

The writer of I Thessalonians tells us that prayer should be such a consistent part of our life that we should **Pray without ceasing (I Thessalonians 5:17).** In other words, we should be so faithful in prayer that there is no beginning and no end. There is no amen, but rather a constant flow, a constant pulling away, an ongoing conversation, incessant, relentless. Spurgeon echoes this call by saying, "We must pray to pray, and continue in prayer that our prayers may continue!"

On two different occasions, Jesus confronts, chastises, and even corrects His disciples' lack of prayerfulness. The first instance took place when they were confronted with a demon-possessed boy presented to them by the boy's father. The father was seeking help! The disciples had nothing. No answers. No solution. Try as they might, they simply couldn't address the weather in this tormented boy's life. Jesus reveals the deficiency in their climate when He declares these kinds only come out by "prayer and fasting." Did you see it? **They weren't power-full because they weren't prayer- full.** The lack of the Kingdom Climate of prayer caused them to come up short when someone needed them. How many of us are empty when we are needed because we haven't filled up in prayer?

> THEY WEREN'T POWER-FULL BECAUSE THEY WEREN'T PRAYER- FULL.

The second moment was in the garden. The lack of a prayer climate in the lives of the disciples resurfaces again. This time, however, it wasn't a sick child or a broken parent that needed their attention. This time, it was a suffering, blood-streaked Savior who needed them, and instead of being diligent or disciplined, they fell asleep. **Jesus makes a prayer request.** Think about that for a second. **God makes a prayer request to man.** Jesus simply says, "Please pray for me." But they weren't faithful in prayer. Beauty sleep was more important than bombarding heaven. Jesus returns and asks the blush-inducing, stomach-turning question . . . "Could you not even tarry one hour?" You can read it like this . . . Jesus says to them, "You let me down when I needed you most. **You were rest-full when I needed you to be prayer-full."** The climate of faithful prayer had not been established in their lives, and the result was a storm of embarrassment and guilt that rolled into the disciples' lives.

I believe Paul admonishes us to pray because He knew that to operate in climate changing authority and power, we cannot live in a prayerless level of life. If we do, then we will be discouraged by the anemic results we experience. One man echoes this truth when he says, "Prayerless people cut themselves off from God's prevailing power, and the frequent result is the familiar feeling of being overwhelmed, overrun, beaten down, pushed around, defeated. Surprising numbers of people are willing to settle for lives like that."

While Jesus was with them, the disciples never seemed to get the faithful in prayer climate right. However, to their credit, at some point in their experiences with Jesus, they grasped the idea that this climate was absolutely necessary if they were going to fulfill the call on their lives. Think about all that the disciples saw Jesus do. They saw Jesus with their own eyes heal incurable diseases, multiply bread, walk on water, bring dead people back to life, and yet, instead of asking Him to teach them to do the miraculous, the only thing they asked Jesus to teach them how to do was to pray. They understood that the key to the incredible things He was able to accomplish found their genesis in His faithful prayer life!

If you are anything like the disciples, then you have probably discovered that establishing the Kingdom Climate of faithful prayer can be difficult at times! You would think that prayer would always be a pleasure. You would think that the opportunity to communicate with God of the universe would be a delight. But let's be honest; being faithful in prayer can be a struggle at times! Why? There is a rather obscure passage that may answer this question for us.

Lamentations 3:8-9 (NLT)

*"And though I cry and shout, he has shut out my prayers. He has blocked my way with a high stone wall."*

The Message translation of this passage probably assists us in understanding the struggle even better.

*"Even when I cry out and plead for help, he locks up my prayers and throws away the key. He sets up blockades with quarried limestone. He's got me cornered."*

Have you ever felt like this? Have you ever felt like God was not only not listening but perhaps was shutting out or throwing out your prayers? Have you ever felt like shaking your fist at God and asking Him why He refused to listen and respond? Ever felt like your prayers were blocked and stopped? I know this has been the case in my prayer life at times.

Heartfelt pleas, requests, cries for help, and desire for direction all seem to hit the sheetrock of the ceiling and bounce right back to me. What I have discovered is that according to Scripture, there are at least three reasons why our prayers are locked up, shut out, and stopped. We have direct control over two of these blocking factors. The third is out of our hands but must still be recognized and factored into the equation of our prayer life!

The first wall that can block and stop our prayers is revealed clearly and multiple times in Scripture.

Psalms 66:18

*"If I regard iniquity in my heart, the Lord will not hear me."* (NKJV)

*"If I had been cozy with evil, the Lord would never have listened."* (MSG)

Proverbs 28:9

*"He that turneth away his ear from hearing the law, even his prayer shall be abomination."* (KJV)

*"God has no use for the prayers of the people who won't listen to him."* (MSG)

Can we blame Him? I know that I don't have a lot of patience when my kids won't listen to me. When they ask my advice and then won't do what I advise them to do, then I can quickly come to the place where I question if I should even bother listening or answering. I bet God often feels this way. When this happens, we really want to shake our fists at the heavens, point fingers in God's face, and accuse Him of letting down on His job. But the truth is this blockade isn't really God's problem; it is ours. The prophet Isaiah puts the ball squarely in our court.

Isaiah 59:1-3 (MSG)

> *Look! Listen! God's arm is not amputated—he can still save. God's ears are not stopped up—he can still hear. There's nothing wrong with God; the wrong is in you. Your wrongheaded lives caused the split between you and God. Your sins got between you so that he doesn't hear. Your hands are drenched in blood, your fingers dripping with guilt, Your lips smeared with lies, your tongue swollen from muttering obscenities."*

**The wall of iniquity** becomes an obstacle to being faithful in prayer. Our own sin blocks our prayers. These passages of Scripture irritate me . . . badly because they remind me that my sin keeps God from hearing me! This means that the silence I am enduring is my own fault.

> I KNOW GOD RESPONDS TO THE CRY OF A SINNER BECAUSE HE RESPONDED TO MINE.

I know God responds to the cry of a sinner because He responded to mine. However, if we believe the Word, then it is those of us who are His children, the saved, that (according to Psalms 66:18) He doesn't listen to if we have regard for iniquity. This reveals an even higher standard of holiness to which the redeemed are held. The Psalmist doesn't say we have committed sin; just regarded it. Regard means to consider. When we consider sin, we construct walls that defeat and stop our own prayers! I challenge you as you do the hard work of establishing a climate of faithful prayer and are suffering in silence that you examine whether or not Isaiah 59 describes you. Perhaps, if we simply repent, get our mind right, and drop iniquity like it was hot, we would at the same time turn the key and release our prayers and find our answers, direction, and provision!

There is a second wall that can block our prayers. This is another wall to which we hold the key. **It is the wall of injury.** Jesus was clear. Jesus left us no room for negotiation. He established it as a ground rule of the kingdom that when you approach the altar, an injury can keep you from being heard! Listen again and carefully to His statement in Matthew 5. Don't give yourself permission to dismiss His instructions. Don't justify injury and block your prayers!

Matthew 5:21-24 (MSG)

> *You're familiar with the command to the ancients, 'Do not murder.' I'm telling you that anyone who is so much as angry with a brother or sister is guilty of murder. Carelessly call a brother 'idiot!' and you just might find yourself hauled into court. Thoughtlessly yell 'stupid!' at a sister and you are on the brink of hellfire. The simple moral fact is that words kill. "This is how I want you to conduct yourself in these matters. If you enter your place of worship and, about to make*

> *an offering, you suddenly remember a grudge a friend has against you, abandon your offering, leave immediately, go to this friend and make things right. Then and only then, come back and work things out with God.*

Isn't it interesting that we typically remember at the moment we begin to approach God? Long ago, seemingly forgotten, insults, painful interactions, and conflicts suddenly resurface as we approach our Father in prayer. Jesus is teaching us that injury between you and someone else can stop your prayers! Injuries interrupt! Some of us suffer in silence because we refuse to do the hard and painful work of reconciliation. Earthly relationships can block your heavenly relationships! Jesus knew that our lack of unity has more bearing on our ability to communicate with God than we realize. So, when Jesus prayed for His followers, His request was that unity would invade their (and our) lives because He knew that without it, they would come to the altar with no ability to hear or to be heard.

The third wall is a wall that we must know exists. However, the removal of this wall isn't always in our purview. The third wall that can hem our prayers in is the **wall of silence**. If you haven't discovered this yet, just hold on because the more time you spend in prayer, you will eventually run headlong into this wall. Silence is a part of prayer. I think one of the biggest mistakes we make when trying to become faithful in our prayer life is that we confuse silence as a lack of response.

God is silent at times because we pray contrary to His will. Our prayer doesn't demand a response because He has already responded in His Word, and we have failed to read or heed His Word. How do you respond as a parent when your kids ask you a question that they already know the answer to? Do you feel compelled to respond? Sometimes, silence is simply God shouting, "I have already spoken!" However, there is another reason for silence, and that is interference. This is what Daniel experienced. In Daniel 10, the Bible details a prayer session in which Daniel prays and doesn't receive any answer for 21 days. An angel appears to Daniel after the three-week delay and informs him that he had been held up by enemy resistance.

The enemy can and will interfere with our prayers. When we experience inference, rather than giving up, we can be encouraged to remain faithful in prayer as we remember the great truth found in Daniel 10:12. Daniel is informed from the moment he humbled himself and began to pray that his prayers were heard! That should encourage us! The enemy may try to intercept and even stop our prayers. It may seem like he has been successful in that endeavor because there are some of our prayers that we have prayed months and, perhaps, years ago that seem to be unheard or overlooked. But Daniel's experience teaches us that those prayers are still alive and still in process! Don't give up. Don't mistake silence for a lack of response! The answer will eventually come! Hold on. Believe. Trust. Walk in the assurance that interference doesn't equal interception. An interception is a turnover. Interception means going the other way and defeat. Interference only equals delay! So, while this wall of silence is out of our control, we must continue in faithful prayer!

As we build this climate of faithful prayer, we must determine whether we are fighting our own prayers by regarding iniquity or injury. Is our prayer blocked by interference? If we discover that our prayers are being blocked by iniquity or injury, then we must step up and tear those walls down. If we find that silence is the culprit, then we need to check our requests against God's Word. If we are praying according to His recorded will and still experiencing deafening silence, then we must realize that our prayer has been heard and we will get a response at the right time. (See I John 5:14-15!)

I often hear believers bemoan their lack of time for prayer. The truth is we all have the same 86,400 seconds in each day. The Kingdom Climate of prayer is established when those seconds are consumed by faithful prayer!

So, grab your baggy pants. Dust off those flashy dance moves. But do more than sing the lyrics. Realize that to make it through this day and to set the climate for the days ahead, we must pray!

# 16. GRIN AND SHARE IT!

**Kingdom Climate Characteristic 10: Share With Others**

It is the very next word. Immediately following the first "da-da" or "mama" that is uttered, you can count on it to be next. It is a word that expresses ownership and possession. It is a word that sets boundaries and marks territory. It is a word that implies a physical response if not heeded. The word that every child learns and utters very quickly is the same word repeated repeatedly by every adult. It is the word "mine." If you ignore that word, it will feel like you have stepped on one! Mine can be spoken in relationship to a toy that another child wants to play with at the daycare. Mine can growled when the parking space opens up in front of the grocery store, and the car that has been sitting patiently with a blinker on is rushed past by the rude person who is self-absorbed and in a hurry. The word is learned early, and the selfish tendencies that come with it can be long-lived in each of us. Paul addresses this tendency in an attempt to uproot it out of our lives. He knows that the tendency to be selfish and only concerned with mine can lead to some nasty weather. Paul implores us to battle for Kingdom Climate by becoming sharers. He makes this statement in Romans 12:13 (NIV), "*Share with the Lord's people who are in need.*" The Message version says, "*Help needy Christians.*" Paul realizes that in order to produce Kingdom Weather, the Kingdom Climate of **generosity** must be established in our lives.

Notice Paul doesn't say to share with those in want. In other words, we feel no compulsion or directive to assist those who buy what they want and then beg for what they need. We are not called to establish a climate that perpetuates and rewards laziness. If you have the latest and greatest phone, weekly appointments to get your nails done, and you're wearing the latest $200 pair of tennis shoes, don't ask me to help you pay your utilities. No . . . Paul says the climate is that we should rally around those in need. This directive also speaks to operating in a climate where we are comfortable enough to share our needs! We can't meet a need that we don't know about. But once the need is shared, Kingdom Climate is that we push back the desire to keep everything as mine, and instead, we are responsive to those in need. We rally to "family" in need. We don't use up everything we have on ourselves. We look for those who are in need, and we respond. Whose need have you met lately? Why do you have extra? Is it to spend on you? Probably not . . . most likely, God has given you more than enough to bless someone else! This isn't even about an organized effort from the platform. This is a way of life where we intentionally make efforts to be sensitive and responsive to the needs that we recognize around us! We should look for needs, knowing that one day, we, too, will need the body to respond to our needs. In order to build the Kingdom Climate of being sharers, we are forced to examine our hearts and attitudes toward possessions.

> WE LOOK FOR THOSE WHO ARE IN NEED, AND WE RESPOND.

The type of Christianity that we have embraced in America draws a huge line of separation between God, the church, and our personal finances. We know about the separation of church and state, but what we practice more diligently is the separation of church and estate. We like to quote Psalms 24:1 (KJV), "*The earth is the Lord's and the fullness thereof*" - or in other words, God owns everything. We like that concept. However, the struggle to share becomes real when He gives some of that fullness to us. Then, we tend to make those things off-limits. Instead of taking stewardship, we want ownership. The struggle begins here because if we see ourselves as owners, then we will want to regard what God has given us as "ours." So, we begin to call it "mine." Therefore, we generally don't hold those things lightly but rather tightly.

That is what happens in Acts 5 when Ananias and Sapphira sell a piece of property and then declare that they are giving it for the good of the gospel. However, the truth is they didn't allow the Jesus they claimed as

Savior to also be Lord. When it came to their stuff, they were fine with lying. You will remember that their separation cost them their lives. We shake our heads at these two, but the truth is most of us will willingly sing songs that state, "I will give you my all only to draw lines around the items that are excluded. We give Him stuff we don't want or like and act as if we have worshipped and sacrificed. We do this, even though David already taught us that unless something costs us, it isn't really worship. How many of us lie about our stuff to God, and because we die slowly, instead of suddenly, we believe we have escaped God? The way we approach what God has given us is broken.

A beautiful young redhead goes into the doctor's office and says that her body hurts wherever she touches it.

"Impossible!" says the doctor. "Show me."

The redhead took her finger, pushed on her left cheek, and screamed; then, she pushed her elbow and screamed even more. She pushed her knee and screamed; likewise, she pushed her ankle and screamed. Everywhere she touched made her scream.

The doctor said, "You're not really a redhead, are you?

"Well, no," she said, "I'm actually a blonde."

"I thought so," the doctor said. "Your finger is broken."

I include this story at the risk of offending all the blondes reading this book (didn't we already deal with that weather?). You may want to know that although it is hard to tell now because everything has turned grey, I am a fellow "tow head." I think the risk is worth it because this fictional account reveals an essential truth. This young lady's broken finger caused her to think everything was broken. I have learned that if I am broken in one area of my life, I am usually broken in other areas as well. If I am broken with pride, then I am usually struggling in relationships. If I am shattered by wanting control, then I am weak in faith. If I am broken in my understanding of stewardship and sharing, then I am usually fractured in the area of generosity and compassion. Brokenness in one area usually produces pain in other areas of our life. There are some foundational truths that will help us shake off the brokenness in this area of our lives and will enable us to live in generosity.

Poverty can be a way of thinking. It is a principle that we learn. We know this because folks with nothing can be happy, and folks with unimaginable riches can be unhappy. Money doesn't correct or fix a poverty mentality. Solomon, who received twenty-five tons of gold a year in addition to the taxes he received from merchants and traders, explained to us in Proverbs 11:4 (NIV) that *"wealth is worthless in the day of wrath."* God is interested in our money and possessions simply because it reveals where our hearts are and what we value. According to Malachi 3, we either value or devalue God by how we handle our money. When we don't value God with our money and things, we want to blame God for our struggle, but He just gets in agreement with what we set in motion.

Poverty is often rooted in fear. It is the fear that I will never have enough. I will never have what I need. I will never have enough to share. We will quote and say we believe David when, as an old man, he states in Psalm 37:25 (NIV), *"I was young and now I am old, yet I have never seen the righteous forsaken or their children begging bread."* However, the enemy attacks our minds so that we fail to truly trust. We allow fear to unseat faith. A lack of trust in one season is usually a revelation of a broken heart in another season. Scripture informs us that we haven't been given a spirit of fear. However, if we have expectations that aren't met like we prefer or if the need of our life seems to go unmet, we have a tendency to pick up a spirit of fear. Our fallback position becomes doubt. You can certainly see this in the area of finances. People who are full of faith in other areas of their lives can slip into doubt, panic, and make bad choices in the area of finances. They fail to trust Him in that arena of life as well.

Poverty is often linked not to a lack of resources but rather to a lack of stewardship. Money doesn't and won't solve our problems, but discipline will. Poverty mentality is broken by planning. This is a partnership that is established with the power of the Holy Spirit. He teaches us to become content. He teaches us to become generous. He helps us become disciplined.

Proverbs 13:18 (GW) tells us that *"Poverty and shame come to a person who ignores discipline, but whoever pays attention to constructive criticism will be honored."* You must learn the skills and discipline necessary to manage what you have, or what you don't have will manage you. We know this is true because someone who is bound by poverty can get a raise, win a lottery, or get a bonus, and, in a matter of minutes, days, weeks, or months, they are back to broke! We get a blessing and don't know how to steward/manage the blessing. When we are bound by poverty, we need food but will get our nails done instead. We need to pay a bill, but we will eat out three times a day instead. Poverty is often learned helplessness. So, in order to break poverty, God doesn't have to increase my finances. All He has to do is convince me to learn stewardship by learning how to budget and save for what I want so that I won't have to beg for what I need. We want God to miraculously change our finances, but He requires us to methodically change our stewardship.

I know that many times, the spiritual and Scriptural practice of tithing is waved around like a magic wand. We want to use it as a way to twist God's arm into giving us more. However, we must learn that you can't tithe your way out of bad habits. Granted, if you tithe, then faithful to His Word, God will bless. However, unless you correct your habits, you will squander any blessing obtained by your obedience. Again, we must learn to think differently. We can't throw the required amount at God as if this gives us license to mishandle the rest and expect Him to rescue us! Tithing is not a magic recipe that makes stupidity disappear. You have heard it said that you can live better on the blessed 90% than you can on the 100%. That is true **IF** you handle the blessed 90% correctly!

# TITHING IS NOT A MAGIC RECIPE THAT MAKES STUPIDITY DISAPPEAR.

A poverty mentality is identifiable by the existence of trouble. How many of us gain what we call "wealth" (clothes, cars, possessions) or "blessings," but our procurement of those things is coupled with trouble? We find ourselves stressed, stretched, controlled, and consumed. Enslaved. By earthly standards, wealthy, but in very real and spiritual terms . . . bound. Wealth obtained by our own hands, rather than obtained as a blessing from God, comes with, and is accompanied by trouble! Listen to what Solomon says in Proverbs 10:22 (TLV), "*The blessing of Adonai brings wealth and He adds no trouble with it.*" Solomon knew that when God gives, there is no trouble that comes with the blessing. What kind of father would "bless" his children with the knowledge that what he was giving them would also result in trouble? Some of us have obtained things we dreamed about, but now, in order to maintain or keep those things, our lives are filled with trouble. I would submit that we obtained a lot of what we call blessings from God on our own; therefore, we have also inherited trouble.

So, in order to build a Kingdom Climate of sharing, we must learn the lesson that Moses tried to teach Pharaoh. In Exodus 10:21-27 (NIV), Moses is instructed to confront Pharaoh about letting the Israelites leave the bondage of Egypt. It is an interesting exchange.

> *God said to Moses: "Stretch your hand to the skies. Let darkness descend on the land of Egypt—a darkness so dark you can touch it." Moses stretched out his hand to the skies. Thick darkness descended on the land of Egypt for three days. Nobody could see anybody. For three days no one could so much as move. Except for the Israelites: they had light where they were living. Pharaoh called in Moses: "Go and worship God. Leave your flocks and herds behind. But go ahead and take your children." But Moses said, "You have to let us take our sacrificial animals and offerings with us so we can sacrifice them in worship to our God. Our livestock has to go with us with not a hoof left behind;* **they are part of the worship of our God.** *And we don't know just what will be needed until we get there." But God kept Pharaoh stubborn as ever. He wouldn't agree to release them.*

Moses, a Hebrew raised as an Egyptian, is called by God as a deliverer to set the children of Israel free from 400 years of slavery and bondage. The challenge is that the Pharaoh doesn't want to give up hundreds of thousands of workers. To get his attention, God uses Moses to deliver ultimatum after ultimatum. In fact, the passage you just read in Exodus is the account of the ninth plague . . . darkness. The issue is that after each devastating plague, Pharaoh would change his mind. This time is no different, except for the statement that Pharaoh makes in response to this plague. Tired of the darkness, Pharaoh summons Moses and says if you will turn the lights back on, then you can go worship. However, there is one stipulation. You can go worship but just leave all your stuff here. Leave all your cattle, sheep, goats, etc. This should inform us that the enemy doesn't mind if you worship as long as you leave broke.

Pharaoh realized that if the people left everything they owned behind, they could go and worship, but it was inevitable that they would come right back into bondage after worship. The enemy of our soul doesn't have many new tricks. This is the same trap he lays for us today. We run to sanctuaries on Sunday. We praise. We worship. We have an encounter with God, but the rest of the week, we run back into bondage because what we do in worship has no bearing or impact on what we own or possess. We have left that in the hands of our pharaoh. But Moses makes it clear to Pharaoh, and to us, that our possessions are part of the worship of our God. So, our livestock, cars, and homes have to go with us because we cannot separate our worship and our stuff. It is as we share that we worship!

Most of us, when we are blessed, never stop long enough to ask, 'Why?". What's this for? Why did God put this in my hands? Why did I get the job? Why did I get the bonus? I believe it is when we discover the "why" that we are able to finally embrace stewardship and learn to share. There are three reasons God blesses us.

First, God blesses us to advance His Kingdom. Through our faithful giving, people in need are given assistance. Missionaries are able to spread the Gospel to places we may never see or even be able to spell. Ministries can afford to lengthen the reach of the message of Jesus' love. Bibles are printed. Hungry children are fed. Medical needs are secured. This list that could go on and on is accomplished by God. However, He accomplishes this with our finances! We literally are partners with Him.

Secondly, He blesses us so that we can care for those for whom we are responsible. There are some that carry your last name, but that doesn't mean you are responsible for them because of the way they choose to live and the choices they choose to make! Likewise, there are folks who don't share your name but who are God's assignment for you. Why do you think your paycheck went further than it normally does? Why do you think the bank let you skip making a payment with no penalty this month out of nowhere? There are those who can't care for themselves and those who will not care for themselves. We must learn the difference. Those who won't care for themselves, according to Paul (2 Thessalonians 3:6-10), are supposed to feel hunger! No interview? No work? No job? Play Station all day? Then feel hunger, baby. **We are not responsible for someone's**

> HE BLESSES US SO THAT WE CAN CARE FOR THOSE FOR WHOM WE ARE RESPONSIBLE.

**irresponsibility.** Did they spend their rent money on a football game? Then we are not responsible for keeping them off the street. They claim they are hungry, but they used their meal money on a movie? Then, let that stomach growl. **However, there are those who can't care for themselves, and God blesses us so that we can share the wealth.**

Finally, God blesses us for enjoyment. But that comes after advancing His agenda and caring for those for whom we are responsible. When we are bound by a poverty mindset, we want to flip the script. That is why the majority of the people interviewed about the meaning of life say it is to have fun. We think it is only about enjoyment. So, we chase fun, and in the process, we find chains. If we had taken care of #1 and #2, then we would have enjoyed the fruit of our labor. Here is a truth we need to know . . . If we take care of #1 and #2, then God will take care of #3. We want God in the mix, but we don't get the order right. We flip the script and then want God to ignore our mismanagement when He requests that we give back. We even go one step further and ask and expect God to give us more when we know (and He knows) that we will squander, waste, and slavishly use the more on us. Too many of us can't respond to #1 and #2 because we are still bound to a slave mentality. We would have given, we would have assisted and responded, but we can't because we just used it all on the eighth TV at home because the other seven were over a year old. We would have been able to help you with food, but we needed to upgrade our phone from a 6.0 to a 6.1 because now we can take pics by tilting the phone a little to the right rather than pushing one button. Moses and Paul want us to live as free men, yet we are acting like slaves. The kingdom suffers, the residents of the kingdom suffer, but, man, have you seen my fourth car? God doesn't want you to be poor. He wants you to be prospered, but we have to handle the blessing properly. I believe God smiles from heaven when we get the order correct and are able to enjoy the trip, the car, the house, the nice meal, or the special activity. Don't you do that when you are able to abundantly bless your kids?

So, I am asking you . . . do you have the script flipped? Are you living out of order? How often does the word "mine" either come out of your mouth or at least cross your mind? If we are going to build a Kingdom Climate, then it is time to recognize just how blessed we are and then grin and share it!

# 17. BELLY BUTTON THEOLOGY

**Kingdom Climate Characteristic 11: Cultivate Hospitality**

Misunderstood? Maligned? Unappreciated? Disparaged? By us? For sure. By Jesus? I don't think so. Jesus has been traveling. He is probably tired from His journey and the constant clamor for His attention and touch. He finds a respite by accepting the invitation of a family that will become one of His closest allies and friends. It was on this first foray into their home for a meal that we get a glimpse into the family dynamics. In that glimpse, we also give one of the women involved a really bad rap. Jesus sits down to relax and recover and then has to correct Martha's focus. The adjustment to her focus is what we fixate on. It is the rebuke that gets our attention. The moment of correction. This focus on Martha's temper tantrum (weather) and Jesus' response causes us to overlook the climate that Martha has established.

Luke 10:38-42 (MSG)

> *As they continued their travel, Jesus entered a village. A woman by the name of Martha welcomed him and made him feel quite at home. She had a sister, Mary, who sat before the Master, hanging on every word he said. But Martha was pulled away by all she had to do in the kitchen. Later, she stepped in, interrupting them. "Master, don't you care that my sister has abandoned the kitchen to me? Tell her to lend me a hand." The Master said, "Martha, dear Martha, you're fussing far too much and getting yourself worked up over nothing. One thing only is essential, and Mary has chosen it—it's the main course, and won't be taken from her.*

Because Martha's moment of panic and frustration is so evident in this passage and because we want to put the necessary emphasis on worship, we tend to throw Martha under the bus. Every preacher worth his or her salt has contrasted the actions and posture of Martha and Mary in this moment. Perhaps we need to take a moment and notice the second sentence of this account. It says that Martha was the one who "welcomed Jesus into her home and made Him feel quite at home." Mary didn't extend the invitation or set the climate of hospitality that made it possible for her to sit at Jesus' feet. Martha pulled that off. Martha orchestrated that moment. Martha is the one who established Kingdom Climate for the King. Granted, her tendency to get caught up in the details of how the table was prepared and the task of making sure they didn't run out of sweet tea (Jesus would have only drunk sweet tea because unsweet tea is from the devil!) got her a literal "come to Jesus" moment. But we can't disregard the fact that Martha's hospitality brought the Son of God into her house.

Haven't you experienced what Jesus experienced? There are just certain people who have this innate ability to make you feel welcome. In a crowded room, they have this way of making room for you. That is Kingdom Climate. Paul admonishes us in Romans 12:13 (NIV) to *"Practice hospitality."* I love how it is written in the Message version . . . *"be inventive in hospitality."*

> **PAUL IS ENCOURAGING US TO BE LIKE MARTHA WITHOUT SUCCUMBING TO STRESS OR ANXIETY.**

Paul is encouraging us to be like Martha without succumbing to stress or anxiety. He is telling us to cultivate hospitality. To become people who look for new ways to help our neighbors feel welcome and at ease. This will require us to go out of our way. This will require us to become more aware of the person sitting at a table by themselves in a crowded cafeteria. This will mean that we approach people in the lobby that no one else is talking to. I am convinced that Paul's instruction will require us to love differently. More than considering our feelings, it will force us to think about how someone else feels in a room, a church, or a worship service.

Over the years, folks who come to our church have complimented the aesthetics of the building, the powerful praise and worship, and, at times, the quality of the messages that are preached. I am always thankful to hear these evaluations. However, I am most thankful that on a regular basis, when people visit, I hear them say that this is the friendliest and most welcoming church they have ever attended. Like most pastors, I want to hear that our church is the most spiritual and anointed. What I have come to learn, and this is hard to admit because I think most pastors want to believe our sermons are the most important thing on a Sunday, is that it is the climate of hospitality that positions people to be receptive to change. The message, although important, can be received or ignored by how people are received when they show up in the building. In fact, the climate of hospitality may even be more important than the atmosphere of worship created by the most skilled worship team. Now, don't get me wrong, I know Jesus elevates worship above preparing the meal. But again, I remind you that if Martha hadn't first established the climate of hospitality, the moment of worship would have never taken place. As a pastor, I have come to this conclusion because I have discovered that if we aren't welcoming, making room for others, and friendly, then the lack of hospitality can literally unpreach the best message I preach. How you look at and treat someone in the parking lot or lobby may be the difference between them getting touched by God or not! Lack of hospitality undermines worship because it builds barriers that people often can't push past to meet Jesus. Be honest, haven't you ever walked into a church as a visitor and felt awkward and out of place because no one spoke or helped you find the kids' ministry for your kids?

Let's go one step further. Let's move it outside the four walls of the church. The same need for hospitality exists, and maybe more so in your school lunchroom or your work break room. There are people everywhere who find themselves on the outside looking in. Longing to be included. Longing to have a seat at the table. A voice in the conversation. People have been marginalized and ignored. People are looking for acceptance and warmth. As believers, we should be the most welcoming and hospitable people on the planet. Our ability to tell them about Jesus may very well be determined by our willingness to act like Jesus first.

John makes it even more blunt in I John 4:20-21 (MSG) when He asks the question, *"If he won't love the person he can see, how can he love the God he can't see? The command we have from Christ is blunt: Loving God includes loving people. You've got to love both."* John makes it apparent that people won't want to sit at Jesus' feet if we represent (re . . . present) Him so poorly in our attitude that they are turned away or turned off. Why would I want what you have or worship who you worship if what you have and who you worship makes you gripey, selfish, unpleasant, scowling, angry, or allows you to consistently operate in a bad mood? I think John, like Paul, recognized that **hospitality is the seedbed for change!** We prepare people for a Jesus encounter by smiling, extending a hand, speaking to them, and making room for them! Too often, those of us who are enjoying time at Jesus' feet forget to make room for anyone else to approach. This is because we live in what is, perhaps, the most selfie-centric (self-centered) generation that has ever walked the planet. The problem is **spiritual people can be self-centered; they just can't be Christ-like.**

Several years ago, I had the privilege of taking a hiking trip in Israel. My guides believed that the only way to learn the land was to walk the land. So, day after day and mile after mile, we walked the ancient paths of the Holy Land. I remember one grueling hike in particular. After an already long day of exploring, our guides instructed the bus driver to enter an area that Jews really aren't supposed to enter. In fact, the bus driver quickly dropped us off and left the area. We walked past a poor excuse for a barrier and began a hurried march on the actual Jericho Road. The sun was quickly setting, and our guides encouraged us to keep up a quick pace along the rocky path. The hike was brutal. It was steep, and it was dusty. To describe the path as narrow doesn't even do it justice. We literally couldn't walk side by side. We could only traverse the path in a single-file line. It was then that I remembered the story Jesus told with this road as a backdrop.

Luke 10:30-37 (MSG)

> *Jesus answered by telling a story. "There was once a man traveling down from Jerusalem to Jericho (14 miles with an ascent of 3,300 feet). On the way he was attacked by robbers. They took his clothes, beat him up, and went off leaving him half-dead. Luckily, a priest was on his way down the same road, but when he saw him he angled across to the other side. Then a Levite religious man showed up; he also avoided the injured man. "A Samaritan traveling the road came on him. When he saw the man's condition, his heart went out to him. He gave him first aid, disinfecting and bandaging his wounds. Then*

*he lifted him onto his donkey, led him to an inn, and made him comfortable. In the morning he took out two silver coins and gave them to the innkeeper, saying, 'Take good care of him. If it costs any more, put it on my bill—I'll pay you on my way back.' "What do you think? Which of the three became a neighbor to the man attacked by robbers?" "The one who treated him kindly," the religion scholar responded. Jesus said, "Go and do the same.*

Like you, I have read and told this story hundreds of times. But while on this rapid march down the actual road, the story suddenly had more meaning. We tend to picture the wounded man lying in the gutters of one of our wide streets. We see the priest and Levite walking down the sidewalk of our neighborhood, spotting the beaten man in the distance, and then casually crossing the street to avoid him. However, this march revealed something different. There is no "other side". There is only the sharp fall off the side of the cliff and the hundreds of feet on nothing but air until you reach the canyon floor below. In other words, when the priest and Levite refuse to get involved, assist, or tend to the needs of this injured man, they have to literally step over his broken and bruised body. No possible argument or excuse is plausible that would lead you to the conclusion that they just missed him or didn't see him. These men chose to step over rather than rescue. They couldn't avoid this man physically. Instead, they created distance between the man and themselves with their attitude.

Paul's list of Kingdom Climate Characteristics includes hospitality so that we won't make the same mistake. We cannot intentionally step over people on our way to worship. We cannot intentionally step over people on our way to success. We cannot look down at the beaten-up people on our way to our place at the table and into our comfortable circle. Instead, we are to go out of our way to make room for people. We cannot buy the lie that the more I love God, the more I will love people. The truth is, when we are growing in Christ, when we are operating in Kingdom Climate, the more we love people, the more we love God.

> WE CANNOT LOOK DOWN AT THE BEATEN-UP PEOPLE ON OUR WAY TO OUR PLACE AT THE TABLE AND INTO OUR COMFORTABLE CIRCLE.

Jesus' hospitality story is a blunt call to lay down our lives for people who are not like us. He could not have chosen two individuals who were more diametrically opposed - socioeconomically, racially, and religiously different. There was absolutely no common ground to be found. The Good Samaritan was good because he was hospitable. This despised enemy of the Jews carries a wounded, almost dead Jew into a Jewish inn. Talk about taking a risk. In old Western terms, this would be like an Indian bringing a cowboy with three arrows protruding from his back into Dodge. Then he goes one step further and leaves him there with an open-ended tab. Jesus' account implores us to become the kind of people who help those who can't help us back. But then, He even says to take it one step further. Help even if, after we help, they still hate us, spit in our faces, and want us dead!

One telltale sign that we are not operating in a climate of hospitality but are self-centered like the priest and Levite is when **we want people to go further than we are willing to go.** So, when "we" are hurt, sick, or missing, we want people to stop their lives, change their schedules, break their routines, stop on the road and call, check on us, chase us down, spend their money on us, use their resources, take a chance, risk it all and pray for us, but when we see others who are hurt, sick, or missing, we are AWOL. We are so consumed with enjoying our encounters with Jesus that we forget to help anyone else get near Him.

I believe that in this instruction to practice hospitality, Paul was simply trying to teach us the "Theology of the Belly Button." Right in the middle of every one of us is a visible reminder that we are connected. We started life connected to someone else who sustained us, fed us, nurtured us, and protected us. It is a reminder that we may be the key to someone else's survival. We are supposed to be attached. We are supposed to be "others" minded. We are each other's lifeline!

Because this climate is so foreign in our society, I think it would be helpful to actually list a few practical ideas on how to practice hospitality.

1. Make a concerted effort in conversations to keep the subject on the other person rather than yourself.

2. Attend church over the next few weeks and months to see someone who needs help and respond. Rather than coming to church for your blessing, I want to encourage you to come to church

to look for God and for people. Don't come just to worship. Show up instead to see someone in pain, hurting, or in need and respond. If you do this, I would venture to say that you will encounter God, and your worship will be deeper and more meaningful.

3. For the next few weeks, go to work every day with an eye toward the fact that God sent you to work to help somebody find help that may never come to a church. In fact, go to work not for money or for your own sense of worth or fulfillment but rather to find the one who is beaten up. Look for the beat-up soul!

4. Find someone to encourage. Target someone! Be intentional.

Do it! I know you want to. Stick your finger in your belly button, remove the lint, and remember, we are called to make room for others.

# 18. YOUR FEET CLEAN?

**Kingdom Climate Characteristic 12: Bless Your Neighbor**

Lies had been told. False statements were made in order to secure advancement. Kindness and grace extended had long been forgotten. Trust was abused. What made it worse was that this had not happened to me but rather to someone I love deeply. My hero had been attacked, and the fallout and impact on this person was severe. A trusted advisor who knew what had really happened approached me in the aftermath and asked me how I was doing. In a less than Jesus-like but candid moment, I replied, "I love Jesus, but I really want to cut somebody."

Have you ever been there? The pain, the attack, the assault, the offense is so great that you want to strike back. You want to defend. You want to set the record straight. These types of situations and moments reveal the fact that this particular Kingdom Climate Characteristic may be one of the most difficult to get firmly rooted in our lives (In fact . . . spoiler alert . . . Paul knew we would struggle with this so badly that he addresses it again at the end of his list of characteristics). Without thinking, we can simply fall back into our flesh and root for the demise of those who wrong us or the ones we love. Paul must have known this because he could have simply instructed us to be a blessing. However, we need to slow down and read his instructions again.

Paul says, in Romans 12:14 (NIV), Kingdom Climate is *"Bless those who persecute you; bless and do not curse."* The Message Version says, *"Bless your enemies; no cursing under your breath."*

Wait. Read it again slowly. We must read it slowly so that it will sink in because the truth is that most of us operate in a pseudo-kingdom Climate. We bless those we like, love, and who treat us properly. But Paul says genuine, weather-changing Kingdom Climate is apparent and in operation when we mature to the place where we actually bless those who either consider us or who we consider to be enemies! One version (CEB) makes this instruction even harder to swallow when it interprets the command as "*Bless those who harass you!*"

> KINGDOM CLIMATE IS WE SPEAK WELL OF THOSE WHO NOT ONLY SPEAK BADLY OF US BUT ACTUALLY PERSECUTE AND HARASS US.

The word "bless" here is the Greek word "Eulogeo," from which we get the word "Eulogy." It means "to speak well of." Did you get that? Kingdom Climate is we speak well of those who not only speak badly of us but actually persecute and harass us. Not only do they talk smack about us, they actually take action to produce pain. Paul says bless them. Think about that for a moment. He is saying that when someone is an enemy, I am to call down the blessings of God onto them! I refuse to do to them what they are doing to me! It is the concept of turning the other cheek that Jesus talks about. When someone strikes you on the cheek, the undamaged cheek is turned away from the attacker. Jesus is saying to expose the unblemished side of the face so that the assailant can now produce pain on that side, as well. This takes restraint. It takes crucifying our natural instinct to strike back. This takes work!

Here is where it becomes even more taxing. Paul's instructions to bless those who persecute us means that I can't even be upset when I see people who are persecuting me experiencing blessing. In fact, because I am operating in Kingdom Climate, I am actually speaking blessing into their lives! I am responsible for bringing their undeserved blessing to pass. So, when a person who is harassing us wants to flaunt their blessing in our face, rather than getting mad, we can take credit. They probably don't even know it, or if they did, they wouldn't acknowledge it, but God is blessing them through us! The truth is they don't have favor . . . it is God's favor on us, produced by Kingdom Climate, which is rubbing off on them! There are numerous examples of this happening in Scripture. The favor of God on Joseph fights off famine for a pagan kingdom. The favor on Esther's life impacted not only her own people but rubbed off on the king, who made her a queen. Three young men refuse to bow to the culture or the idol of a king, and the favor on their life causes this king who tried to cook them to honor the One true God. This is just another reminder of how important and strong climate really is. The Kingdom Climate in our life creates weather in people we may not like and who don't like us! When we operate in Kingdom Climate, even our evil boss will be blessed . . . why . . . because we work their office!

In order to graduate to this level of living, we must learn as believers how to handle offense. We must learn to establish an offense-defense. We need this defense because offense isn't optional. Jesus Himself makes it abundantly clear that as long as we are breathing, there will be things that offend us. He tells us this in Luke 17:1 (KJV), "*Then said he unto the disciples, It is impossible but that offenses will come: but woe unto him, through whom they come!*" Offenses will come. It is impossible that they won't come. Therefore, we shouldn't be shocked when they come. We should be prepared, and we should know how to respond. I think this idea that we can live life unoffended has given birth to a lack of preparation and being equipped to properly handle, address, and endure conflict. So, when someone treats us badly, we not only don't know what to do, we certainly aren't prepared to bless them. Jesus makes it a point to tell His disciples that they are going to be offended! Why should you expect anything less? In fact, He says offenses (plural). It isn't going to be one-and-done. He wants us to understand that part of life is being offended. Now, just to be clear, He also condemns the one who causes offense. So, He isn't giving the offensive person a pass. Instead, He is teaching us to be mature enough to deal with offense appropriately.

The Greek word for offense that Jesus uses is "skandalon," from which we get the word "scandal." The word originally referred to the part of the trap to which the bait was attached. So, offense is nothing but a trap to entangle and strangle us. It is an attempt to steal our peace, our emotional energy, and our focus. What Jesus is telling us is that traps aren't optional; being trapped is! The trap is dangerous because, as John Bevere's incredible book, The Bait of Satan, teaches us, "An offended heart is the breeding ground of deception."

Paul's instruction in Romans 12 isn't his only instruction regarding being hurt by others. He addresses it again when he writes to the believers in Ephesus.

Ephesians 4:26, 31-32 (TLB)

> *If you are angry, don't sin by nursing your grudge. Don't let the sun go down with you still angry—get over it quickly, for when you are angry, you give a mighty foothold to the devil. Stop being mean, bad-tempered, and angry. Quarreling, harsh words, and dislike of others should have no place in your lives. Instead, be kind to each other, tenderhearted, forgiving one another, just as God has forgiven you because you belong to Christ.*

The truth is that "forgotten grace" breeds "unforgiving living." Some of us struggle to handle offense simply because we have conveniently forgotten how much forgiveness has been given to us.

I am reminded of Jesus' instructions to His disciples as He sends them off to practice ministry. He tells them to enter the villages around them and attempt to share the good news with the people who live there. But remember, Jesus knew that offense was possible, so He anticipated that these fishermen-turned-preachers would have doors slammed in their faces. They would be unaccepted, rejected, turned away, ignored, and probably ridiculed. Jesus prepares them, and us, for this type of unwarranted and unnecessary treatment. In Matthew 10:14 (CEB), Jesus says, *"Shake the dust off your feet as you leave that house or city."* Jesus is literally saying to them and us that we should not allow the residue of their actions to gather on us. We can't let their anger towards us, their bad words about us, their attacks against us slow us down or stop us in our walk. Instead, we establish a Kingdom Climate and bless those who persecute us. So, the question must be asked . . . "Your feet clean?"

# 19. YOU DON'T LOOK GOOD IN GREEN!

**Kingdom Climate Characteristic 13: Uproot Jealousy**

A man was driving his Yugo (if you are not familiar with the Yugo, then do yourself a favor and Google it!) when he pulled up next to a Rolls-Royce at a stoplight. The driver of the Yugo rolled down his window and shouted to the driver of the Rolls, "Hey, that's a nice car. Do you have a phone in your Rolls? I've got a phone in my Yugo!" The driver of the Rolls looks over and says simply, "Yes, I have a phone."

The driver of the Yugo says, "Wonderful! Say, do you have a refrigerator in there, too? I've got a fridge in the back seat of my Yugo!" The driver of the Rolls, looking annoyed, says, "Yes, I have a refrigerator."

The driver of the Yugo says, "That's wonderful! Say, do you have a television in there, too? You know, I have a TV in the back seat of my Yugo!" The driver of the Rolls, looking very annoyed by now, says, "Of course, I have a television. A Rolls-Royce is the finest luxury car in the world!"

The driver of the Yugo says, "It's a very cool car! Say, do you have a bed in there, too? I have a bed in the back of my Yugo!"

Upset that he did not have a bed, the driver of the Rolls-Royce sped away and went straight to the dealership, where he promptly ordered that a bed be installed in the back of the Rolls. The next morning, the driver of the Rolls picked up the car, and the bed looked superb, complete with silk sheets and brass. It was clearly a bed fit for a Rolls-Royce.

The driver of the Rolls began searching for the owner of the Yugo. After searching all day, late at night, he finally found the Yugo parked, with all the windows fogged up from the inside. The driver of the Rolls-Royce got out of his magnificent vehicle and knocked on the door of the Yugo. When there wasn't any answer, he knocked again and again and again. Eventually, the owner of the Yugo stuck his head out, soaking wet. The driver of the Rolls stated condescendingly, "I now have a bed in the back of my Rolls-Royce." The driver of the Yugo looked at him in disbelief and said, "You got me out of the shower for that?"

> WE ARE SO CONSUMED BY WHAT EVERYONE AROUND US HAS THAT WE CAN'T EVEN ENJOY WHAT GOD HAS GIVEN US.

This is how many of us live our lives. We are so consumed by what everyone around us has that we can't even enjoy what God has given us. Everyone's perfect, social media-cropped, and edited life captures our attention, and we miss, overlook, and often despise the Rolls-Royce quality life we have been given by our good, good Father. Our hearts become full of a destructive disease called jealousy. This sickness is so deadly that it caused an angel who had been given charge of all the worship in heaven to become so dissatisfied with his position that he attempts to overthrow God Himself so that he can take the throne. If jealousy will impact an angel's place in heaven, then surely, we must make the conclusion that jealousy can destroy us here on earth!

Paul states in Romans 12:15 (NIV) that we should "*Rejoice with those who rejoice.*" In other words, I don't despise you when you are blessed. I don't look at your blessed job, marriage, kids, and life, and secretly wish I had your job, your spouse, and your life. Paul says we should put ourselves in each other's shoes so that when you are blessed, I rejoice. I will throw a celebration party when you get something I don't have. I will cheer your promotion even if I haven't been promoted in a decade. The only way to live in this type of Kingdom Climate is to battle and ruthlessly uncover and uproot jealousy from our hearts.

Kingdom Climate is destroyed by jealousy because jealousy turns compassion into competition. Jealousy causes us to see anyone below us as unworthy or unnecessary. Those above us are not only the misplaced standard, but they also become the mistargeted enemy. I have to knock them off. I have to outdo them. I have to outget them. I have to unseat them. It is hard to love one another when we are jealous of one another!

Don't think those near Jesus can't be overcome by jealousy! I remind you of the scene in Luke 22 where we see the holy, righteous, revered, anointed, favored apostles/disciples sitting together, and this statement is made . . . "Now there was also a dispute among them, as to which of them should be considered the greatest." If that wasn't bad enough, in Matthew 20, John and James' mom comes and bows down at Jesus' feet and begs that her sons be given the seats of favor when He becomes king. The other ten disciples hear this request being made and get angry. These are the disciples, mind you. They are with Jesus minute by minute, and yet, they are jockeying for position! They are so green with jealousy that two of them even get good ol' Mom to come fight for them. Jealousy seeps in, and it is deadly. These guys are rubbing shoulders with Jesus, and this reveals that jealousy doesn't even have to make sense.

We are told in Scripture that God is a jealous God. His jealousy will consume you. He won't share us with anyone or anything else. If that is the case, then why don't we realize that jealousy from the enemy can also consume us? Please note that there is a difference between the jealousy of God and the jealousy of the devil. God's jealousy is healthy for us because His jealousy is protective. It keeps us focused on and solely committed to Him. The jealousy of the enemy will destroy you because it is possessive. It controls us! Too many of us are being controlled by this sickness. Our attitude. Our outlook. Our words. Our heart. All are being controlled by jealousy. That is jealousy from the enemy.

Jealousy is a dream killer! If you are pursuing or jealous of someone else's dreams, you can't pursue your own dreams. If you are filled with jealousy, then you are going to have a difficult time loving the calling you have. You will spend all of your energy and time loving the calling you wished you had. If you are filled with jealousy, then you won't love the spouse, the kids, the job, the car, or the house you have. Instead, all of your attention will be used up on the spouse, kids, job, car, or house you wished you had! Some of you can't accomplish your own dreams simply because you are so jealous of someone else's dream. We often think we are just greedy. However, there is a difference: Greed wants more, and jealousy wants theirs!

For some reason, we play like jealousy is just a mild, manageable, and normal climate. It would do us good to remember the weather that jealousy produces. Read James 3:16 (NASB) slowly and let it sink in. *"For where jealousy and selfish ambition exist, there is disorder and every evil thing."* Think about that statement. This passage reveals that jealousy is really ugly and dangerous. Jealousy is an ingredient for a climate that makes room for every evil thing. Jealousy is literally an entry point for the enemy to access my life! Jealousy is the launching pad. The passage declares that it is a certainty. There is no maybe or perhaps. It simply assures us that if there is jealousy, then there will also be chaos and evil things going on in our lives.

We need to know that jealousy is rooted in fear - fear that I will miss out if they get what I want. Fear that if they are more talented, then they will get the role or the response. Fear that I will be overlooked. The solution is understanding what II Timothy 1:7 (NKJV) tells us! *"For God has not given us the spirit of fear, but of power and of love and of a sound mind."* So, if we are jealous because we are filled with fear, and God hasn't given us the fear, then who is the author of the fear? The enemy. Paul tells us we have not been given fear. We don't have to operate in fear. We can live in the knowledge that our Father knows what we need and that He is working for our good! We don't have to be afraid, so we don't have to be jealous. So, if we turn green, and most of us do, then how do we change the climate? How do we learn to live with those around us that cause us to be jealous?

Because our natural inclination or conclusion is that if I am going to be able to beat jealousy, then I am just going to have to disconnect from everyone and live separated from everyone. But remember that earlier, we discovered that Kingdom Climate is achieved through connection. Jealousy is defeated not by a lack of relationship but by a lack of attention. In other words, I can defeat jealousy if, while I am connected, attached, and in relationship with you, I allow the Holy Spirit to capture my attention so that it isn't focused on you, your blessings, your gifts, or your abilities. Each hand does what it does best. Each hand gives its gift. Each hand receives its reward. My right hand can excel, shine, and get applause, but my left hand doesn't get jealous because it isn't focused or paying attention to my right hand. We are connected, in relationship, but we are no longer in competition or fighting for attention. I focus on my hand. I am not distracted by your hand! I know Kingdom Climate is being established in my life when I learn to celebrate God's goodness, even when that goodness is given to someone else!

Let's stop and ask some climate-revealing questions. Are you applauding in public and attacking in private? Are you wishing for and even plotting destruction on someone because they have what you want? When was the last time you celebrated someone's prosperity, even when it meant you missed out? When was the last time you celebrated someone's promotion when it meant you were passed over? When was the last time you rejoiced over someone else's raise when it meant you had to wait another year? Maybe a card or email celebrating someone's success could be sent. Perhaps pick up the phone and tell the person on the other end of the line just how proud of them or thankful you are for their gift or their contribution to your life. These simple steps have profound implications for them, but they are also a preventive medicine for the jealousy that tries to take root in our hearts.

It is time to examine our wardrobe. You look stylish in that bright blue shirt. Those beige pants are becoming. That red number is stunning. But let me give you some fashion advice . . . I mean climate advice . . . you don't look good in green!

# 20. MAJOR VS. MINOR

**Kingdom Climate Characteristic 14: Embrace Empathy**

There were only a few minutes left in the end of the third period. I was sitting on the baseline, keeping stats of my oldest son's performance just like I had in every middle school and high school game of his basketball career. However, this particular game was different for three distinct reasons. First, he was a senior, and every game meant we were one step closer to the end of this incredibly enjoyable experience. Second, this was a national basketball tournament at the end of the school year. The push for a national trophy was high stakes and high pressure. The third reason this game was different was because as the seconds disappeared from the game clock, I suddenly felt a sharp pressure in my chest. I hadn't eaten anything for breakfast, and this was a relatively early morning game. I had grabbed a Dr. Pepper from the concession stand on the way into the gym and figured the early morning carbonated drink was causing me to have a case of heartburn. The pain and pressure continued until the game ended. My son wanted to stay and watch the next game. So, I decided I better get something to eat to stop this intensifying ache. However, after the breakfast sandwich, the pain only grew worse. So, while my son watched the next game, I hopped in the car and drove to the drugstore for some antacids. After downing half the bottle, I still had no relief. Finally, I went to a secondary gym and tried to lie down in the stands to see if that would help. Nope! Finally, I texted my son and said, "We have to go." Surprisingly, no argument! He simply helped me as I struggled to the car for the 45-minute ride back to the hotel.

At the hotel, my parents tried to convince me to go to the nearby hospital, but I didn't want to be a distraction to my son's tournament, so I flatly refused. I thought I just needed to lie down on the bed, but as soon as my head hit the pillow, the pain in my chest began to radiate up my arm and ultimately climbed up the side of my jaw. That was enough... I finally agreed to let my parents rush me to the emergency room. When we entered, the staff hurried me back to a room for an examination, only to discover that I was having a heart attack at 46 years old. I will never forget what the cardiologist, who inserted a stent into my heart, told me after the procedure. He stood over my hospital bed and said to me, "If you had waited any longer, this would have been catastrophic, but, thankfully, it was only a minor heart attack."

> IN MY CONDITION, STRUGGLING WITH THE REALIZATION THAT I WAS JUST MINUTES AWAY FROM DEATH AND LEAVING BEHIND MY WIFE AND SONS, I HAD THE REVELATION.

It was there, lying in a hospital bed with tubes and needles coming out of what seemed like every limb and all kinds of machines and alarms beeping in the background, that I learned the difference between major and minor. In my condition, struggling with the realization that I was just minutes away from death and leaving behind my wife and sons, I had the revelation. It was easy for the doctor to describe what I had just experienced as a minor because he wasn't feeling what I was feeling. However, this was major for me. Therein is the difference . . . it is major if it is happening to me, but only minor if it is happening to you.

Paul, in the second half of Romans 12:15 (NIV), says, *"mourn with those who mourn.»* He is trying to convince us to cultivate the Kingdom Climate Characteristic of empathy. This climate totally dispels the idea that things are only major if they are happening to us. In fact, what Paul is trying to get us to do is to feel what those around us are feeling. When those around us are in the depths of despair, disappointment, or agony, then we shouldn't think it is a minor deal. We should, instead, mourn with them over the major loss they are experiencing, even though the same calamity hasn't reached our house.

As I have matured, a fancy way to say gotten older, one of my favorite passages of Scripture has become John 11:35. Jesus has been waiting, and even delaying, for four days after receiving news that Lazarus was sick. By the time Jesus joins His friends Lazarus is dead. When He arrives on the outskirts of town, Martha comes out and expresses her disappointment in Jesus' absence. She basically has a "Come to Jesus" meeting with Jesus and gives Him a piece of her mind. Then, she goes home and tells Mary that Jesus wants to see her. Mary approaches Jesus. Her approach is described differently than Martha's. The passage says that as Mary walks towards Jesus she is weeping. She is devastated by the loss of her brother. John tells us that when Jesus saw Mary weeping, "Jesus wept." Many love this verse because it is easy to memorize. Just two words. I love this verse because it shows us that Jesus felt what Mary was feeling. This verse is so easy to memorize, but it is much more difficult to emulate. To operate in empathy, we must place ourselves in the shoes of someone else and feel what they feel. It requires us to take the attention and focus off of our own lives, our own schedules and successes, and put ourselves in their shoes. We must consider their emotions! Jesus exhibits this climate throughout His earthly ministry. On at least six different occasions, Jesus is said to have been moved on by compassion when He sees people struggling and hurting. He felt them.

Matthew 27:34 (KJV)

*"There they offered Jesus wine to drink, mixed with gall; but after tasting it, he refused to drink it."*

While hanging on the cross, the most painful method of execution devised by man, Jesus was struggling to take His next breath. He was rapidly losing fluids as He strained against the pain, stripped to the bare minimum of clothing, in the heat of the sun. Finally, mustering all of His strength, He is able to gasp, "I am thirsty." The soldiers hear the statement and take a branch, attach a sponge to the end of it, and soak it in a mixture of wine and gall. They extend the branch to the thirsty Savior, but He refuses to drink. Why? Why didn't Jesus sip the cocktail to relieve His thirst and recover some of the fluids He had lost? Scholars believe that the wine and gall concoction would have acted as a type of pain relief medication. In other words, this drink would have numbed Jesus to the pain. I believe Jesus ignored His own thirst because He didn't want anything to dull His ability to feel what we feel. He dismisses the opportunity to diminish the weight of our sin that was dropped on His already heavy and bleeding shoulders. He wouldn't lessen the excruciating pain of separation from His Father so that He could empathize with us when the decisions we make produce division between us and God. Right in the middle of His worst moment, Jesus displayed the most incredible example of this Kingdom Climate characteristic!

> OUR SOCIETY TRIES TO GET US TO GROW NUMB. WE CAN WATCH DISASTER, NOT ONLY WITHOUT FLINCHING BUT WITHOUT FEELING.

Our society tries to get us to grow numb. We can watch disaster, not only without flinching but without feeling. We see families lose everything in a storm. We watch friends have their lives ripped apart by divorce or death, and if we are not careful, we go on with our lives, never feeling for them. Jesus, our perfect example, showed us a different way. Even when we are experiencing pain and disaster ourselves, we can have an eye, an ear, and a heart turned towards the anguish of those around us.

Paul realized that when the Kingdom Climate is constructed in our lives, the weather of our lives will change. Now, he wants us to look around us and see that just because our waves have leveled out and our ride has become more endurable, it doesn't mean everyone else is experiencing the calm that we enjoy. From the safety of our blessings, what our neighbor, friend, classmate, coworker, or family member is facing may seem like a minor deal to us. But that is only because it isn't happening to us. Paul wants us to elevate the feelings and experiences of others so that we are able to feel them!

Our own physical body illustrates how this is supposed to work. Here is your assignment . . . if you choose to accept it! Go get a hammer, rearback, and hit your thumb as hard as you possibly can. That is the easy part of the assignment. Here comes the difficult part! Try to convince the rest of your body to act like most of us react to those around us in pain. Try to get the rest of your body to ignore the pain in your thumb! If you accept this challenge, then please video it and put it on social media for the rest of us to enjoy. You know, as well as I do, this isn't possible! When the hammer descends and meets the flesh of your outstretched thumb, every nerve ending in your entire body is going to explode with a variety of responses. Your feet will feel the hurt, and try as you might, you won't be able to help it; you will have to hop or dance. At that same moment, your eyes will become a waterfall of cascading tears. We will probably also need to turn down the volume on the social media post you make because the pain will shoot out of your thumb, up your arm, across your shoulder, into your jaw, and, ultimately, find its way into your tongue. Words you didn't even know that you knew will have to be held back!

Welcome to the Kingdom Climate of feeling what others feel that Jesus practiced and Paul instructs us to build in our lives. It is alive in us when our entire body responds in the good moments or the bad moments to our brothers' and sisters' experiences. Their major is no longer our minor. Instead, their smashed thumb, wrecked car, totaled marriage, unruly kid, pressing bills, and anxious mind are the signs that they are lying on the hospital bed and their heart is at stake. We may not understand what they feel. We may have never experienced it ourselves. We may even conclude that if they would make an adjustment here or a tweak there, they could escape or change what is causing the pain. But before we offer advice. Before we list the steps to freedom. Before we quote Scripture. Weep with them and feel!

# 21. SANDPAPER AND SONGS

**Kingdom Climate Characteristic 15: Nurture Harmony**

You have probably heard of me. In my younger years, I was in a band. That's right, I was onstage, front and center, with my instrument rocking out. OK, before you try to look me up on Pandora or Apple Music or before you get the image of me with long flowing hair, wearing spandex, and killing an electric guitar stuck in your head (What, you don't see me that way? If I weren't practicing Kingdom Climate #12 of Blessing - I would be totally offended right now.), let me be honest. I was in a band . . . a booster band. Some of you probably have no idea what a booster band is. In the old days, all of the children in the church would be handed various classroom instruments such as the triangle, the sticks, or my personal favorite . . . sandpaper blocks. We would then be paraded to the church platform on Sunday morning, and we would, usually poorly, sing and play a few catchy little children's church songs to the delight of apparently hard-of-hearing folks with no musical taste! We would belt out classics like "I'm in the Lord's Army" and "Deep and Wide." However, there is one particular song that we sang, probably complete with a sandpaper block solo, that Paul would have loved. The lyrics of the song simply said:

> If we all pull together, together, together. If we all pull together how happy we'll be! For your work is my work, and our work is God's work; If we all pull together. How happy we'll be!

Man, I feel like grabbing some sandpaper, a couple of blocks of wood, and hitting the concert tour!

The song was simple and silly. However, it also taught us the Kingdom Climate that Paul mentions to us in this increasingly difficult list. He says in Romans 12:16 (NIV), "*Live in harmony with one another.*" Realizing this may be a challenge at times, he says it again. In the second mention of this characteristic, he uses the little two-letter word, an overlooked word also found in the song. Romans 12:18 (NIV) "***IF*** *it is possible, as far as it depends on you, live at peace with everyone.*" Paul says, if it is possible, live in peace knowing that the Kingdom Climate's characteristic of harmony would calm many of the waves in our lives. He is teaching us to pull together.

Notice that Paul puts the ball in our court. He says, *"As long as it depends on you."* He doesn't say, "Stay in harmony based on someone else reciprocating your efforts. Stay in harmony if the other person makes it easy." No, again, he says, "As long as it is possible with you." It puts the responsibility of creating and maintaining a climate of peace and walking in harmony squarely on our shoulders. The way Paul writes this makes it clear that he knows that we will run into someone who won't accept the harmonious relationship we are offering. He knows that there will be moments when we will do everything within our power to get along with someone, and they will refuse to participate in peace. But at the end of the day, Paul paints us into a corner and says we must do our best regardless of whether the other party does their best to keep the peace! Then Paul really makes it difficult because he adds one word to the statement. *"Everyone!"* If he had excluded the folks from the other political party, then this command would have been so much easier. If he had allowed us to withhold harmony from the people who are of different skin color, social status, culture, or belief system, then the climate of harmony would have been a cinch. But Paul says this climate must be extended to everyone!

Paul says Kingdom Climate dictates that we do everything in our power to keep harmony. Here are some ways to do that: walk away, bite my tongue, keep my opinion to myself, resist my anger, and give up my right to the last word! **In other words, work harder at keeping peace than we do destroying it.** In our day, it seems that we actually work harder to make it possible to stay in turmoil, to stay angry, to stay heated than we do to live in harmony. We choose to use certain words or major on certain topics when we post, knowing that it will stir up controversy and contention, though we also know it won't really produce any change. We seem to take pride, or at least joy, in creating contention. We take particular and planned actions that we know ahead of time will disrupt peace. We often justify this by thinking we didn't start it, but we are not keeping harmony if we keep it going once it is started! It would help us to remember that Proverbs 6 tells us that there are seven things God hates. One of those things Solomon lists is a person who is constantly stirring up strife. I am convinced that too many of us stir stuff up to make ourselves feel more important, or we have become so used to strife, chaos, and turmoil that we will create it or keep it going just to make things feel normal. Proverbs says God hates that. Paul says the result is bad weather. We never stop to consider our part in keeping the peace. Then, for some reason, we are shocked when storm clouds show up on the horizon of our lives!

If you haven't found this, you haven't lived long enough. There are some people who are easier to be in relationship with than others. Jesus discovered this to be true. He had certain people that He spent more time with and became closer to than others. There is nothing wrong with that reality. However, in our attempt to operate in Kingdom Climate, we must be careful, or **we allow our preferences to turn into prejudices.** Over the years, I have watched so many believers become imprisoned by their own preferences. The result is broken harmony. The preference for a particular style of music. The preference for a particular color of carpet. The preference for a particular style of preaching. The preference for a particular group of people. Preferences turn into prejudices that result in broken, fractured relationships. No, willingness to budge. No willingness to compromise. No willingness to work at peace. In order for us to enjoy Kingdom Climate, we must come to a place where we are no longer loyal to, prejudiced towards, fighting for, or promoting any other culture but Kingdom Culture. In the words of the song sung by Israel Houghton, "This isn't a white thing, black thing, male thing, or female thing. This is a kingdom thing!"

> JESUS HAD CERTAIN PEOPLE THAT HE SPENT MORE TIME WITH AND BECAME CLOSER TO THAN OTHERS.

In the Old Testament, a statement is made that should cause us to fight harder for harmony than just about anything else. In a society that seems to relish the idea of constant bickering and constant conflict, read this chapter in Psalms very carefully.

Psalms 133 (KJV)

> *Behold, how good and how pleasant it is for brethren to dwell together in unity! It is like the precious ointment upon the head, that ran down upon the beard, even Aaron's beard: that went down to the skirts of his garments; As the dew of Hermon, and as the dew that descended upon the mountains of Zion: for there the Lord commanded the blessing, even life for evermore.*

Another version translates that last statement like this . . . *"that's where God commands the blessing, ordains eternal life."*

Hold on! Wait just a second. We need to think carefully about this harmony concept. The writer makes it clear that unity/harmony is like the ointment that ran down Aaron's beard onto the skirts of his priestly garments! Wow! So, then, couldn't we conclude that one of the reasons we often fail to operate with the anointing of the Holy Spirit in our lives, families, circles, and maybe even our churches is that there is no climate of unity or harmony? Our lack of peace breaks the flow? If that is the case, and the writer makes it clear that it is, then harmony should be one of our chief concerns. However, the writer doesn't stop there. He reveals the incredible impact this climate change can have on our lives. He says that the climate of unity/harmony actually comes with a guaranteed blessing. Read the last line of the chapter again. In Scripture, a commanded blessing is attached to only one place. That place isn't church. It isn't a worship service. It isn't a room where everyone agrees on every topic or issue. Instead, a commanded blessing is guaranteed to fall on the lives of those who fight for, work for, struggle for, and do everything in their power to keep peace with those around them. So, we have a choice: we either do everything we possibly can to make harmony possible and experience a commanded blessing, or we can stir stuff up and experience God's hate! It is all about the climate WE create. If we all pull together, then our work becomes God's work!

Break out your hidden triangle skills. Dust off your kazoo. I will bring my sandpaper blocks. It is time for a Booster Band reUNION Tour (Get it? reUnion. Come on, keep the peace and say that you did!)!

# 22. CROSSING THE LINE?

**Kingdom Climate Characteristic 16: Avoid Pride**

"I dare you! I double dog dare you!" It is over at that point. You have no choice. With the utterance of the pinnacle of all challenges, you have to do whatever it is that you are dared to do. I can remember, in one of the few instances in my childhood where I was involved in a "fight," that the double dog dare culminated in a stick being taken by my adversary and a line being drawn in the red dirt of West Oklahoma. The "fight" that followed after I stepped over the line was nothing more than some pushing and shoving. However, that moment taught me to think carefully before I step over lines.

I think Paul stops in his increasingly difficult list to draw a line in the sand. The line is a fine line. He wants us to know who we are in Christ -to be firmly rooted and established in our "Christ-like" identity. This new identity gives us the necessary confidence to walk boldly and powerfully in our "joint heir" status. Paul knows that if we aren't careful, as the weather changes with each additional step in establishing Kingdom Climate, we get closer to the line. If we are not careful, we will cross it, and, in most cases, we are not even aware we have done so. The line Paul points out is moving from confidence into conceit. Paul bluntly states in Romans 12:16 (NIV), "*Do not be proud.*" He even doubles it up (maybe it is a double dog dare?) by ending the same verse by saying, "*Don't be conceited.*" He knows the tendency in this journey towards climate-sustained weather is to move from knowing that the source of our new weather is ultimately Jesus to beginning to believe that we can produce this change on our own. We begin to act like we are the source. We have the power by the work of our hands to make this happen. Paul dares us to stay on the right side of the line by carefully avoiding being filled with pride that would separate us from others who are still suffering the stormy seasons in life.

I also think Paul keeps adding items to the list because He recognizes the connection that exists between these issues. He knows that in order for us to cast aside jealousy, establish empathy, and live in harmony, we can't have pride. In order for Kingdom Climate to become a reality, we must let go of pride. Pride is a two-sided knife. It can make you elevate yourself in your own mind so that you aren't mindful or careful of others. You become too good. But pride has another edge that cuts; pride keeps you from allowing anyone to know when you are hurting. Pride forces us to live life behind masks. We become caught up in appearances and what people may think. It keeps us from being vulnerable and real, and, ultimately, it robs the rest of the body from being able to respond. Pride will isolate us. It makes us suffer in storms while acting like we are experiencing perfect weather. We just can't be real.

It would help to remember that pride is one of the seven deadly sins. Perhaps it is the base ingredient that produces the rest of that vile list. It is certainly what caused the only weather delay in heaven. Perhaps this is why the prophet Isaiah used the word picture of "lightning falling from the sky" when he described the fall of Satan. I can see the gathered thunderclouds as this most historic lightning strike takes place. Satan allowed pride to take root in him, and the hurricane of rebellion and punishment was the result. Pride produces the same weather in us.

We should already know that pride is destructive. It is one of the things that Solomon tells us that God hates. It is ironic that so many of us allow pride to take root and then pray for God to ignore or tolerate what He hates. That equation doesn't work any more than it does to ask a parent to take their belligerent child to get ice cream. No parent in their right mind will reward a rebellious child with a trip for a sweet treat. The climate we desire can't exist if pride is present.

If God's stated hate for pride doesn't get our attention, then perhaps the Scripture that tells us God actually resists the proud should be a stark wake-up call. Think about that statement for a second. To have the life, marriage, career, family, and climate we so deeply long for will require God's constant and consistent assistance. However, if we allow pride to become a part of our climate, God literally works against us. Yikes! We know what happens when we work against God, but this is an entirely different level of destruction. Now, the most powerful force in the universe and beyond brings His power to bear against us. This produces a fall. Pride travels ahead of us and paves the way to a fall. Dreams fall. Plans fall. Peace falls. Joy falls. Therefore,

> PRIDE TRAVELS AHEAD OF US AND PAVES THE WAY TO A FALL.

pride must be ruthlessly uprooted. This must be done because pride causes us to unseat God from His throne. Our opinion, our truth, and our judgment are given more weight, more credence, and more importance than His. As we sit down on His throne, the insidious and ultimately deadly aspect of pride is that revealed pride may be one of the most difficult issues to recognize in our own lives. If we are proud, then we come to the conclusion that we alone are right. This paints us into a corner where we not only resist but dismiss all correction. Course correction that leads to climate correction becomes increasingly difficult. It causes us to set ourselves up as judge and jury. It causes people who have been forgiven much to forget that graced people should be gracious people. William Law had it right when he said, "We love humility and we hate pride only in other people. Never once in our lives have we thought of any other pride other than that which we saw in other people. The fuller of pride anyone is himself, the more impatient he will be at the smallest instances of it in other people."

It is interesting to me that Paul waits so late in the list to mention this issue. I am convinced it is because as we follow his instructions up to this point, we begin to reap the benefits of the changes we have made. Paul knows that it is at that moment that we become susceptible to pride and the devastating fact that it can destroy everything that has been accomplished up to this point. Pride takes root, and we take credit. Then the storms come back, but our pride won't let us admit that we messed up. Nor will pride allow us to repent. We walk around with smiles on our faces, a strut in our steps, and a storm in our hearts. We just don't let on that the weather is back. We are more concerned about our reputation than we are about our climate. Sixteen characteristics in, we are challenged to reassert our reliance on Jesus in this journey. Without His help, strength, power, and Climate-changing authority, we don't stand a chance.

Since Paul already double-dog dared you, I triple-dog dare you to take a careful examination of your heart. Is there pride there? Has the temptation to take credit for your better days led you to believe you did this? D. L. Moody was most accurate when he said, "I believe that the moment our hearts are emptied of pride, selfishness and everything that is contrary to God's law, the Holy Spirit will fill every corner of our hearts." Andrew Murray may have said it best when he said, "Pride must die in you or nothing of heaven can live in you." And I would add . . . including heaven's climate. We need to insert patience into our interactions with those who are suffering.

# 23. LET IT GO, LET IT GO!

**Kingdom Climate Characteristic 17: Take No Revenge**

It is that song that you can't get out of your head. It sets up residence in your mind, and without even thinking, you find yourself humming the tune. It becomes annoying. But try as you might, you can't stop. Several years ago, a song set up residence in the minds of young and old alike. This tune instructs us to "let it go." Sorry! I know you are singing it now, too. Have fun with that for the rest of the day!

I am pretty sure that Paul would not have been a big fan of Disney. Maybe that is why I like him so much! I prefer shows with live actors to cartoons. However, I am pretty sure Paul would have loved the song from Disney's *"Frozen."* The anthem "Let it go!" captures the heart of the last Kingdom Climate characteristic Paul shares, which is "no revenge!"

No revenge means that I am so determined to be a blessing and create a climate of blessing that I don't hit back. It isn't that I can't hit back. It is that I make a conscious decision and choice not to do so. It isn't that I can't think of anything to say. It is that I choose to control my tongue! The choice "not to" is what makes me a stronger person in this area.

**I just need to remind you that although we may be on the jury, we are not the judge.** We don't get to carry out the sentence. When we take revenge, it is a revelation of our lack of trust in God. We think we have to take matters into our own hands. And what is worse, we open ourselves up to getting back what we dole out. When we try to do God's job, we shouldn't be surprised when it circles back around, and the revenge we sow is the revenge we reap. Listen, some of us can't bless because we are consumed with revenge. We literally spend hours plotting the demise and rehearsing the destruction of the one who hurt us. The "I will say this next time" and "I should have said this" way of living will keep you in bondage. Your desire for revenge means the truth is the only person in captivity is us. Paul says let bygones be bygones. Paul is telling us to be a fan of "*Frozen*" and "Let it go!" **He understood that the climate of revenge produces the weather of anger, ulcers, insomnia, and sickness! Quit fantasizing about the pain you will inflict.**

In the Old Testament (2 Samuel 2:23), when King Saul was killed, Abner, his cousin, rushes to put Saul's only surviving son, Ish-bosheth, in place as king instead of David. A skirmish between Abner's men and David's men takes place. Abner's men are killed, and he runs in retreat. David's commander, Joab, had a younger brother who was a fast runner. He pursues Abner as he tries to escape from the battle. Abner doesn't want to hurt Joab's brother and begs him to quit chasing Him. Asahel refused. Realizing he had no chance to outrun him, Abner defended himself and, in the process, killed Asahel. Joab was eaten up with revenge and plotted. Two years later, after David had brokered a deal with Abner to gain control of all of Israel, Joab convinces Abner to meet him for a private discussion. Under the guise of a private chat, Joab murders Abner in revenge (2 Samuel 3:27). The revenge costs Joab his life. After David's death, his son Solomon becomes king, and, realizing that Joab was a man of spite and blood, has him killed (2 Kings 2:29-34). The slow boil of hurt and hatred in Joab turns him into a murderer and then, years later, costs him his life and legacy. Revenge will do that to us, as well.

Paul weighs in at the end of this recipe for climate change with a rather lengthy appeal to not get caught up in plotting the demise of someone who has wronged us. In Romans 12:17-21 Paul says:

> *Do not repay anyone evil for evil. Be careful to do what is right in the eyes of everyone. If it is possible, as far as it depends on you, live at peace with everyone. Do not take revenge, my dear friends, but leave room for God's wrath, for it is written: "It is mine to avenge; I will repay," says the Lord. On the contrary: "If your enemy is hungry, feed him; if he is thirsty, give him something to drink. In doing this, you will heap burning coals on his head." Do not be overcome by evil, but overcome evil with good.*

Paul says that Kingdom Climate means that we learn to leave room for God's wrath! It is inevitable on this journey that there will be times when someone mistreats us. An unkind word. A betrayal. A knife to the back. It is human nature to want to strike back. In fact, it is very easy to get caught up in planning these persons' demise. Long hours can be spent thinking about what I could do or say to inflict pain on the person who has hurt me. The truth is they deserve it. And it is for that very reason that we often end up frustrated because it doesn't seem like the person who did us wrong is experiencing any of God's wrath! Perhaps the reason they don't experience any wrath from God is because there is no room left for His wrath. All the space has been eaten up by our wrath. If we would back off and rest in God's ability to defend us, then we would live in peace. God makes us a promise that He will repay. He will avenge us.

Our pursuit of Kingdom Climate forces us to take a different tactic. We offer those who have hurt us what was offered to us by the ONE we so often hurt . . . grace. Paul gives us the playbook to avoid plotting. He gives us the remedy for revenge. He says that we maintain Kingdom Climate when we feed them to frustrate them. We literally freak them out with our goodness. It disarms them and frees us from taking up arms to exact an ounce of blood. The climate of evil produces the weather of evil. We overcome the weather of evil with the climate of good!

In another very familiar statement by Paul, found in Galatians 6:7 (NIV), he tells us that *"a man reaps what he sows."* This passage is where preachers usually land when they are ready to preach or teach about finances. But the truth is sowing and reaping isn't just about money. Paul realized, when Jesus said in Matthew 7:2 (NKJV), *"With the measure you measure it shall be measured to you."* that this sowing and reaping thing went much deeper than dollars and cents. It also dealt with how we treat those who have hurt us intentionally or by accident. Jack Hayford calls this the "**Law of Self-administered Return**." Some of us cut ourselves off or limit our lives because we limit what we give when it comes to relationships. We want to apply this law to our money, but we want to ignore it when it comes to our marriage. We want it to work on our nickels but ignore how it relates to our neighbor. We want it to work in our economics but want to act like it doesn't apply to our enemies. We want to measure wrath, revenge, and harsh words to them. We forget that if we measure them by that measure, then we can't expect to receive grace. We determine how much grace we receive by how much we give. Our return is determined by our willingness to give grace according to the measure we have received.

Paul understood that, like it or not, somebody, even a fellow believer, would come along, rub us the wrong way, say something, or do something stupid. He knew we would have our fair share of opportunities to be offended. In response, he teaches us to approach every relationship with a willingness to make allowances.

Colossians 3:13 (NLT)

*"Make allowance for each other's faults, and forgive anyone who offends you. Remember, the Lord forgave you, so you must forgive others."*

He drives home the point that grace receivers should be grace givers. You can't do this and plot for and dream about revenge at the same time. Jesus goes even further and says, "We should bless those who spitefully use us." Wow, that is an entirely different level. It forces us to grow to the place where we literally pray a blessing on those who mishandled us. When we drive past the car dealer who cheated us, when we walk into the local grocery store and bump into the person who lied about us, when the coworker took credit for our idea and gets a promotion, when the one who smiles to our face and then takes every private opportunity to run us down; when we go out of our way to make someone else's dreams come true only to have them try to destroy ours; Jesus says to bless them. Even after all of the hard work of establishing Kingdom Climate, this is still a difficult task. We must learn to turn them over to God and let Him choose to bless or curse. We rest in the fact that it is His job and not ours. Our actions toward the people who sell us out (Jesus experienced that), lie about us (Jesus experienced that), harm us (Jesus . . . Well, you are figuring this pattern out, aren't you), return evil for our kindness (do I have to write it?) will determine if storm clouds gather or calm seas will prevail.

At 46 years old, running three miles a day, it was unexpected. Over forty years into a relationship with Christ would make it seem even more unlikely. But there I was in a hospital bed after suffering a heart attack. The cardiologist said it was stress-induced. I admit that it was climate-induced. I was overwhelmed. I was filled with turmoil. There was nothing calm inside of me. My world seemed to be crashing down. Ministry was taking its toll. People I had given and given to had made tragic choices, and the fallout blew into my spirit. My back seemed to be constantly hurting from what were unexpected blades of betrayal. Hope and dreams shattered in seconds. It was the perfect climate for a storm. That storm almost killed me. I wish I could say I figured it out quickly. That wouldn't be the truth. I had to come back to these final instructions by Paul and learn to let it go. I could fight back. I could attack. I could demand restitution. I could continue to be hurt, angry, and bitter. Finally, in a moment of desperation, I remembered God's question to Samuel as he mourned the rejection of Saul as King (1 Samuel 16:1). God basically asked Samuel, "Why are you crying over spilled milk?" Asked another way . . . "Why are you mourning over what I am finished with?" At that moment, I was able to let it go, and it finally let me go. As I wept before God, I let the Holy Spirit wash the pain out of my heart. I had to be willing to let Him unearth the pain, bitterness, and regrets, and I placed them on the altar and gave them to God. It was like a switch was flipped. In my heart and my mind, I moved on and was able to remember what had happened without remembering what it had felt like. I was whole, and the storm inside of me quieted down. I finally let it go!

Why don't you? I know you think striking back will feel good. I know you think saying the words you have been planning will bring relief. I know you think laying the trap and springing it will bring satisfaction. The truth is it will only bring storms. If you want to fight, then fight for Kingdom Climate. If you must strike, then strike the bitterness out of your heart. If you must speak, then speak peace to the waves, and they will die down for lack of wind.

## 24. DIG IT!

All the food had been distributed. Julie and I got out of the back of the truck and into our car. We drove the twenty-five miles back to our home, shocked into silence by the destruction we had just witnessed in Moore. We arrived home, but the winds of that May tornado had done more than just impact a city a few miles away. It impacted our minds and hearts. We realized that we, too, live in "Tornado Alley!" The path of that storm could just have easily detoured into our neighborhood and our street. This forced us to come up with a plan. We had talked about it before, but after seeing what we had just seen, there could be no more delay. We began saving and shopping for a storm shelter to install in our home.

We soon discovered that there are several kinds of shelters. There is the one you install in your backyard. We knew this wouldn't work for us because you have to brave the rain and the hail to reach it. There is a company that will retro-build your closet into a safe room. The cost to do so would have created a whole different kind of storm, so we passed. The third option was a unit that is upright and free-standing and is placed in the corner of your garage. We measured and knew we just didn't have the extra room. Finally, we opted for a rather unique version. The model we purchased and had installed goes under the garage floor. You literally park your car over the top of it. The price was paid, and the delivery date was placed on the calendar.

The company arrived. We moved our cars out of the garage. The workers used a large diamond-bit cutting blade and cut through the concrete in the garage floor. They then took a small backhoe and scooped out the dirt under the floor until it was deep enough to lower a steel box that had a sliding door on the top of it. Once the box was in place, they poured concrete around it to secure it. If a storm ever comes our way, then all we have to do is slide the door open, climb the steps down into what honestly feels like a casket, close the door behind us, and wait out the storm. Now, if an F5 tornado like the one that hit Moore comes near where we live, our house may be damaged, but our lives will be spared.

## WE MUST ALLOW THE CLIMATE-CHANGING JESUS TO UNEARTH SOME THINGS IN US.

I started thinking about the installation of that storm shelter as it relates to what has been addressed in this book. To provide us with a safe place in the storm, the workers had to dig out enough dirt to place the shelter. They, in essence, dug us to safety. That same process is what must take place to establish a Kingdom Climate. We must allow the Climate-Changing Jesus to unearth some things in us. He will dig us out of isolation and connect us to His body. He will expose our selfish consumerism and prod us to serve. He will uproot shallow expressions of love and lead us into sincere love. He will till up our tendency to fixate on the evil in people and help us begin to believe the best about them instead. He will put the plow to our wishy-washy ways and help us to become genuinely loyal. Jesus will break up our self-centered ways and help us to learn to give honor where honor is due. He will bore through our depression and pain and fill our hearts with steadfast joy even on stormy days. He will take a shovel to our lack of compassion and mercy and make us patient with those who are struggling. He will scoop out the shallowness of our prayer life and cultivate a "prayer-full" lifestyle. He will sift through the self-absorbed tendencies that we have and will replace them with a sharing, hospitable, and blessing spirit. He takes a bulldozer to the jealousy that has taken root in us and instead fills us with empathy. He will dislodge pride so that we can live in harmony with others and never seek revenge.

The installation process in our garage was messy and painful (just ask my checkbook). The same is true for the work Jesus does in us. There will be fallout and things to clean up. There are cringe-worthy moments when things that were hidden are brought to the surface. But what I learned in my garage is that the process had a worthy end goal . . . safety. In my own life and in the church that followed me in this process, I can testify that it was all purpose-full! The hard work, the self-examination, and all the tears shed as shovel after shovel of stormy soil were removed from my heart, and our church birthed a change of climate. Jesus literally dug us to safety.

Mark Twain supposedly said, "Everyone talks about weather but never does anything about it!" He was right except on one account. He apparently lumped Jesus into that "everyone," and the truth is, Jesus can do more than just talk about our weather. Jesus is willing and able to change the climate of our lives that is creating the weather. The million-dollar question that you must answer as you finish this book is this . . . will you let Him dig in?

# ABOUT THE AUTHOR

Steve began his ministry in 1990 after graduating from Southwestern College of Christian Ministries. He moved to McColl, South Carolina, where he served as Youth Pastor for almost 2 years at McColl First Pentecostal Holiness Church.

In 1991, Steve married his wife, Julie Yeargan Ely. They then moved to Greenville, North Carolina, to accept the position of Youth Minister of the First Pentecostal Holiness Church, where they served successfully for 6 1/2 years.

In September 1998, Steve and Julie returned to Oklahoma, where Steve accepted the position of Director of Student Admissions and Director of Spiritual Life (Campus Pastor) for Southwestern Christian University. Julie served at SCU for 11 years as the Chair of the Music Department and the Director of the college music outreach group called One Voice.

In September 2000, Steve was named National Youth Director of the International Pentecostal Holiness Church. He served in this position for seven years, working with Bishop Doug Beacham and Bishop Talmadge Gardner. While in this role, Steve received his Master of Ministry Degree from Southwestern Christian University.

Steve's first book, The Hidden Hinges of Youth Ministry, was published during his tenure.

In August of 2007, Steve and Julie planted Passion Church in Oklahoma City. In turn, there have been two Pasion Iglesia Campuses born out of this ministry, along with one daughter church. Julie, after eleven years as an elementary school teacher, is once again serving as the chair of the Music Department at Southwestern Christian University and Director of One Voice.

Steve and Julie have two sons: Talmadge, who is married to Kelley, and Devin.

In June 2023, Steve was named as the Director of Clergy Development for the International Pentecostal Holiness Church.

**To learn more about Steve Ely and *Climate Change* and for additional resources, please use you smart phone to scan the flowcode below to visit:**
https://www.truepotentialmedia.com/steve-ely/

www.ingramcontent.com/pod-product-compliance
Lightning Source LLC
Chambersburg PA
CBHW070455100426
42743CB00010B/1622